ABOVE AND BEYOND

Second Edition

Other Books by

Mark A. Biggs

Operation Underpants – 2016

ABOVE AND BEYOND

Second Edition

Mark A Biggs

mbkbooks

MBK CONSULTING

Copyright

Copyright Mark A. Biggs – 2016

Paperback ISBN: 978-0-9924293-7-9
E-Books ISBN: 978-0-9924293-6-2
All rights reserved

No part of this publication may be reproduced or transmitted in any form or by any means, electronic or mechanical, including photocopying, recording, or any information storage and retrieval system, without prior permissions in writing of the copyright owner.

A CIP catalogue record for this book is available from the National Library of Australia.

First Published in Australia 2014

Second Edition February 2017

By

mbkbooks
MBK Consulting
5 Elizabeth Close
Drouin Victoria 3818
Australia.

www.mbkconsulting.com.au

Dedications

In memory of all those who have gone before and those who will inevitably follow, killed in the service of their country – to the kingdom of their God.

Acknowledgments
The Right Reverend John McIntyre, Bishop of Gippsland, Victoria, Australia. For writing the words on prayer.
Peter Bickmore BEM, Royal Navy Costal Forces Veteran
Royal Navy Costal Forces Veterans – www.cfv.org.uk

Photographs
HMS Scylla, courtesy of the Imperial War Museums IWM FL 2932
HMS King George V, courtesy of MaritimeQuest www.maritimequest.com
MTB 243, courtesy of Peter Bickmore BEM
HMS Dasher, courtesy of Tony Drury www.royalnavyresearcharchive.org.uk
Carless Talk Cost Lives poster – Imperial War Museums (PST 0142)

MAPS
Russian Convoy Map, courtesy of naval-history.net
Mediterranean Map, courtesy of naval-history.net

Cover Design
Craig Braithwaite, aussiepics www.aussiepics.com.au

Laurence Walter Biggs

Summary

Above and Beyond is a biographical tale which encourages us, as ordinary people, to value and write of our contribution; to share those special and unique stories fashioned during what is our short stay on this earth.

This is a story of a journey to God that starts in World War Two on the Russian convoys to Murmansk and includes top secret covert operations which, to this day, are still denied. It becomes a promise to serve God, made in the freezing waters of the North Sea in December 1944, after the sinking of MTB *243*.

The Reverend Laurence Walter Biggs lived to fulfil his promise and became an ordained minister in the Anglican Church in England and then Australia. With the revelation that Christianity is only one of many paths to God, his story should have ended. Yet the stories from the past can, for many families, define and influence their own journey, but have you ever wondered, what *is the truth*?

Russian Convoy Map

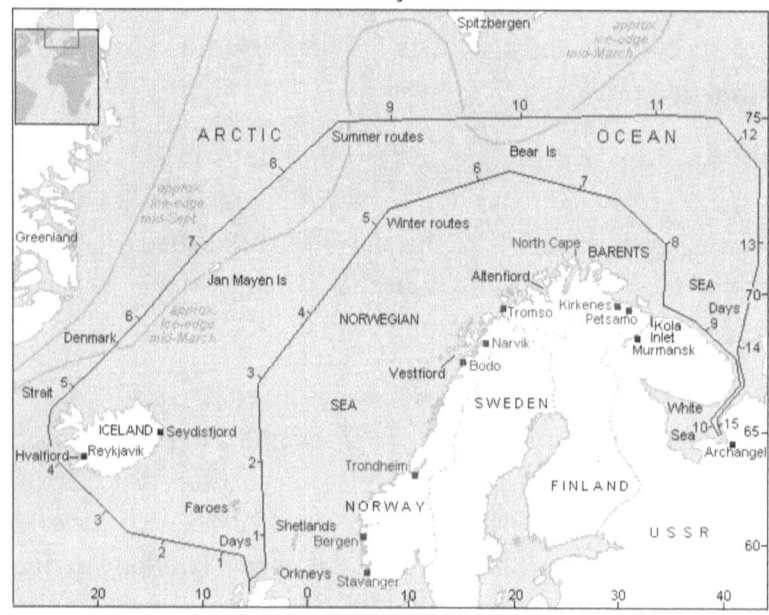

Prologue

Except for those who have had the experience, it is almost impossible to understand the feelings of a young man, in his late teens, standing on the deck of a warship in time of conflict. The wind howling, the ship rolling and pitching and the intensity of the extreme cold eating away at you. There is the relentless nagging feeling of the ever-present danger from mines, torpedoes and all the other hazards of the sea and air. Recently out of school, a boy who after only ten or twelve weeks training is still completely unprepared for adulthood. Now on the flagship, a British cruiser, escorting Merchant vessels carry their goods from America, Scotland and other parts of the world to their destination in the Soviet Union, Murmansk.

The stories of those who had sailed the Russian convoys before could not prepare him for the journey ahead. The majestic power and spectacular beauty of the Arctic or the horrific carnage unleashed by the machines of war which touch the vulnerability of a man's soul, and will be forever etched into the memory.

On board the vessel there's the difficulty of mere survival. Five hundred men living closely together in a ship of little over six thousand tons. On the mess deck, there is the stench from vomit that pools and then flows in all directions, slave only to the motion of the ship. Foul and putrid air is an exotic spice which penetrates and clings to the whole being, escape from which can only be found on deck. But there the cold is an extreme that words cannot describe, so the stench becomes a welcome friend away from the icy exterior. The ship pitches and rolls as if it were a toy and tremendous waves tower above the smoke stacks. There is a fatigue born out of a complete lack of sleep yet an adrenaline inflamed consciousness. Four hours on duty, then four hours cleaning the ship, and then four hours back on duty before a little sleep of two hours. Then it's back on duty for two hours and then maybe another four hours' sleep. The routine and the boredom is broken only by hostilities so deadly and accompanied by a helplessness so complete - as ships and men ablaze sink to the frozen depths.

PART 1

Chapter One

The Story Begins

Laurence Walter Biggs

It's a most beautiful spring morning in Brandy Creek, Australia. The sky is a radiant deep blue and a transcendent almost mystical sound was coming from the birds. I felt at peace with the world. My mind began to wonder and like many people touched by war, I asked, "have I done enough?"

There are many who would say that I was privileged because I was sent to a private, or to use the old British term, public school. Rather costly and rather exclusive, particularly in the context of the era. We were however not upper class, but of the new and emerging middle classes. Influenced by the first war, and then the death of my brother from illness, my parents decided that what wealth they had was to be spent giving me the best education and opportunities possible. This privilege however was not extended to my sister as was the practice at the time. She had to make her own way and would eventually earn a Master's in Speech Pathology.

The old British public school system was the pathway to becoming an officer, a leader in law, business or industry. Despite this conservative education and upbringing, I had in my conscience, a little pink thread, a conviction for social justice. Now I don't think I was ever a communist, but I harboured a nagging inner voice which couldn't quite understand why some were to have and some were not. Why an old-school tie may in some cases be more powerful and influential than a person's abilities.

When I left school, I felt in many ways I had been knocked and cheated by the system. I went to a private school with many famous people, but I was most certainly not famous. When I compared myself to others, I felt of little importance, or at least, for quite a long time, I thought I was. I read recently in the old-school magazine where they had published one or two articles about the early days of the war and gave a list of people from that time who later became Knights of the Realm or held other very high positions such as fellows of the royal society, judges, admirals, air marshals and other people of note. I was not one of those and for a long time, I was conscious that I was not, as our school magazine recounted, 'a person of significance.' And to be honest, I did at moments, covet title and recognition.

It's funny how often we rate our lives and see successes as the titles we gain, the positions we hold, or the possessions we have. As our time on this earth draws to a close, you begin to realise it's not what you have but the journey itself which is important.

The true measure of success is the values by which you have lived your life, the kind of person you have been. A part of success can be the things you have, but it is how you have obtained those things and what you do with them, which are truly important. The question of success then is, "has yours been a principled life, giving service to others?" In truth, we all are important, but at those various junctures in life, we can struggle to distinguish between what is truly important, as our measures become corrupted and betrayed by comparison.

When our time has ended and those we love gather to remember us, if we are genuinely and sincerely honest with ourselves, we want to be remembered for who we were, our character, not what we had or the title we held. Were you a person of integrity, kindness, generosity, love, faithfulness and, were you there in those moments of need?

Now, in my twilight years, the revelation is enlightening if not scary. Have I lived a good life? Did I fulfil my promise? Is there more that I could and should have done?

Since the war, I had carried an overwhelming desire to live a full and spiritual life because I lived when so many died. It is now over sixty years since it all happened and you would think the memories would have grown dim with time. But on a cold winter's night, when the wind is howling and you are tucked safe and invitingly into your bed, the mind drifts back to those days. You live it again in dream and thought, not in a distressed or tormented way, but you are forever being drawn to that most amazing of revelations: I survived and I am still alive all this time afterwards.

If I were to tell my story, which in part would be about war, I would be uneasy that the true character of the journey would be lost. It may read as a glorification of battle, a great adventure of heroic exploits and deeds. At the time, we were all young men, and it is true, there were moments of great excitement. Yet fear, tragedy, and anguish were never far away.

I once read a beautiful passage in a book by Peter Scott, *The Battle of the Narrow Seas* that gave me comfort if I was ever to put pen to paper. It speaks to those who may, many years later, read stories such as mine and see it as a glorious adventure:

> *To him I would say this:*
>
> *That when war comes to a country there is only one course for its people to take, and that is to fight as hard as they can until it is won… or lost.*

That it is necessary for the sacrifice, the unselfish and continuing effort and the heroism of deliberate courage to be recorded so that it cannot ever be forgotten.

That the strain, discomfort and boredom which are the three predominant factors in modern warfare cannot be brought into their true perspective in a book of this kind, or it would be so long and dull that nobody would read it.

That there is no glory to be had out of war that cannot be had out of some greater and more creative enterprise.

That nothing will ever compensate us for the men we have lost, not even the way so many of them died. They were ready to die because they wanted to save their children and their children's children from future war. The least and the most that any of us can do is to devote ourselves to finding complete and lasting peace, and then to maintaining it with all our energy.

I remember my father, Walter Biggs. Born in 1889. He served in World War One and died aged 88, in 1977. Over his life time he must have seen such rapid social, political and technological change. From women gaining the right to vote, to the first Female British Prime Minister. Gas lighting to electricity in the home. The first aeroplane, space flight, and then to watch man walk upon the moon. What interesting stories he had to tell, all of which are now lost. I wish I had asked so many more questions and that either he or I had recorded his journey so that I could pass those chronicles to my children.

A religious book, *The Apocrypha*, isn't taken by all denominations to be complete scripture. In fact, there are some who reject it as just good literature, and yet its words are wonderful, clear, and it is one of the world's most beautiful religious pieces of writing. The word 'apocryphal' has come to mean hidden things, hidden truths.

After all these years, if I were to tell my story it would be an apocryphal version of what happened because I would not do any research. I have no notes, no diaries, just memories from events long passed. A few years ago, when I returned to my native England, buildings I recalled as large now seemed small. Long distances, after the vastness of Australia, seemed short. My friends looked old as I am sure I did myself. The recollection of the truth was still my truth, but was no longer the truth. My story then, if I were to tell it, would be a true story - the truth of my recollections and as seen through my eyes. Memory can sometimes be like a fine wine, maturing and developing with time, they may become more complex, crisp and beautiful, or totally lose its body and refinement - becoming a shallow representation of what it once was.

I wonder then, if I were to write my story and people were to examine the words, whether they may say, *I have a far more interesting story to tell*. I'm sure people do. Maybe then my book would encourage them to commit their account to paper - or whatever the more modern day equivalent is. I think we should record our lives so that those who succeed us - those who gather at our time of passing and, maybe a very much wider audience, will know the true you and the journey you have travelled. For just as we are of this generation, soon we will be the past generation and the stories, the memories of us, will fade gently with time, to be lost and forgotten forever.

My yarn would be about an ordinary sailor who felt privileged to become a Leading Seaman and then eventually a priest in the

Anglican Church. It would be a tale of a journey to a deeper faith and understanding of God, which in many ways, started in December 1944, a Sunday shortly before Christmas as I struggled for life, floating in the freezing waters of the North Sea. The account would end as I near the time of my own death with nightly visits from friends long since departed. The men with whom I served and who like so many others, did not live to see the end of the war.

Chapter Two
Absent from History

Visiting England, I returned to my first parish as a priest in the diocese of Truro, Cornwall. After theological college, I was appointed as a curate of a small county parish in Cornwall, England. Normally, you are curate to the priest-in-charge, but there was no priest and as curate, I was left to run the churches. While visiting St Mary's Sheviock, one of my old churches, I noticed the board of the names of ministers who had served at the church since the 1800s. For the period during which I was in the care of the parish and taking its services, the notice board was silent. No record of anybody between 1968 and 1973, even though I was there for some of those years.

We lived in Tideford (Wilmar House, Church Road) then Crafthole (Sydenham House) and my children went to Landrake primary school. The public record while technically true, as I was not the 'priest-in-charge' and therefore, not entitled, or having the position and authority to appear on the board, gave the impression that during that time, nobody was in the care of the parish, even though I had been there. According to the notice board, and perhaps then, in the fullness of time, it would seem as though I was never there. It made me think about my life and the lives of ordinary people. The people who were there and without whom things wouldn't happen but, because of circumstance, never appear in the records. Although absent from history, they have none-the-less, a remarkable story to tell, yet a story that may remain forever untold.

Did I need my name to appear on the notice board? Perhaps not, but a name on a board does tell a story and its absence another. Maybe it's a reflection of the insecurities of life, but for some reason, a letter, a medal, a salute, a thank you, gives comfort for hard work done and for the small but mighty contributions we all make.

Thinking of Sheviock leads me to remember the day when I received a little piece of paper with the words 'Above and Beyond the Call of Duty' written on it, and a little box containing oak leaves. One may feel proud for being Mentioned in Despatches (MiD), but in truth, you were doing what had to be done, or were just a captive of circumstance. For on any day, people at war go above and beyond, but their deeds and remarkable bravery pass unnoticed - perhaps hidden by the ferocity and mayhem of the moment. Then at another time, a deed, which may be greater or smaller than the things done before, is noticed by those who report such matters and you are recognised.

The story resonates in my memory because of the circumstances surrounding my oak leaves, where just I and two others were the lone survivors of a ship and how this was to colour the rest of my life. It was to be the start of my journey to Christ through the church - although I didn't realise it until several years later, when I became absolutely and utterly convinced that above and beyond us all is a greater power. If there isn't a greater power, then nothing that I have done and nothing that I have thought or believed in would really make any sense.

St Mary's Sheviock - Notice Board

1851	Henry Carew Glanville
1900	Gerald Pole Carew
1910-19	Herbert John Blanchard W
1919-54	Bertie Lycette Lycette
1955-65	William Hall
1965-8	Bernard Walter Benskin
1973-82	Geoffrey Harper
1983-93	Humphrey York
1994-2000	Kenneth John Piper

Chapter Three
Simple Letters

I received some letters and maybe they stirred my pride - but again I was drawn to reflect upon my journey. I would hope not to sound too boastful if I were to tell you what was in them, but the letters and my trip to England reminded me that in their own way, everybody's life is extraordinary.

The first letter touched my heart and triggered dormant memories from the war. It evoked a mixture of both sadness and warmth. The letter was headed 'Embassy of the Union of Soviet Socialist Republics' and on the other side, presumably, those same words written in Russian. This is what it said:

Dear Mr Biggs:

> I have the honour to inform you that the Presidium of the Supreme Soviet of the USSR has awarded you the Commemorative 40 Years of Victory Medal in the great patriotic war of 1941-45. Conveying my personal congratulations on that occasion, I wish to extend to you an invitation on behalf of (and the name is spelt out) the Ambassador of the USSR and the State President of the Victorian branch of the RSL, to come to Melbourne for the ceremony of presentation of the Medal which will take place… etc.

And so, I attended the presentation. Standing there along with several other people you hear your name called. The Ambassador stands in front of you, pins the medal to your chest and whispers in a voice that only you can hear "You know, we consider you a hero of the Soviet Union." Then retreating one step, with great respect gives a slight, almost unnoticeable bow. I wasn't prepared for his words let alone the immediate swelling of emotion which followed. It was a truly touching moment. The criterion for receiving the medal was having endured battles in defence of the Russian homeland. I, along with the other still living survivors, was awarded the medal for my service in the Arctic, the Russian convoys. Maybe, as I gather my thoughts in preparation to write this story, I will reflect on what it was like as a young man, barely out of school, to be on those Arctic convoy runs in and out of Murmansk.

I have never been overly left or right-winged, but down the centre in many ways; conceivably a social conservative with my principles of social justice and free trade, but 'a hero of the Soviet Union'? Receiving the medal made me feel proud, but I was also moved with a strong and imposing sadness of loss. Do you know that over twenty-three million people from the Soviet Union died in defence of their country? Not long after the ceremony, I wrote to the ambassador, thanking him for the presentation. I said that after the war I had always been interested in the affairs of the Soviet Union.

As a surviving World War Two British sailor, having sailed the convoys, the medal awoke a sense of the enormity of the task. Without the loss and determination of the convoy sailors who kept the only supply line open through the Barents Sea, allowing Russia to hold firm against Germany, perhaps we would all now live in a very different world. But I also remembered that, had it not been for the supreme sacrifice of over twenty-three million soldiers from the Soviet Union, (not much short of the entire population of Australia,) maybe the task of defeating Germany would have been a little too great for the rest of us.

How proud I was this year on Anzac Day, at our local war memorial here in Australia, when I was chosen to lay a wreath in honour of those who died in the Great Patriotic War of the Soviet Union.

Standing in silence at the war memorial, your memories are filled with the past and the dreams you had for a future after war. A future which is now all but lived. As the sun shone and its light shimmered from my medals, I looked down upon my ribbons, the bars, and the oak leaves and now underneath, the V-shaped ribbon of the Soviet Union medal. I thought I would feel depressed, perhaps sad, but you know, I don't think I ever felt so proud. Maybe it was because I survived the Arctic convoys, or the thought of the soldiers who died fighting with us, the incomprehensible number - an estimated fifty to eighty million who died during the war. I don't know. But I am pleased that, in my lifetime, the Iron Curtain became a thing of the past and I really do hope it remains a thing of the past.

Fate creates curious friendships and with the wearing of the Soviet medal, I genuinely feel that I have a great link with so many people whom I will never meet and whose politics I may never understand. Murmansk, the Artic and the Barents Sea became for me a symbol of the hardship and brutality of war. At other times, when long after the war, the world and events seemed overwhelming, I remembered Murmansk. Many people feel moved to make a pilgrimage to places that signify or try to give meaning to war, or to other things of great significance in their lives. For me, it's Murmansk, and she still calls.

There was once a time when I feared I would be seen as a warmonger for wearing my medals and remembering Anzac Day. It appeared that our history, the heroism, mistakes and sacrifices made by older generations were to all but fade from consciousness. But in recent times, Australia has found pride in its past. Gallipoli and Anzac Cove in particular, have come to represent both great sacrifice and acts of forgiveness for our wrongs in war. It is the words to be found on a monument at Anzac Cove that I find most compelling; a famous excerpt from one of the speeches by Mustafa Kemal Ataturk, the father of the Turks. They are words of true love, healing and generosity. Could we have said this to people who had invaded our lands?

> *Those heroes that shed their blood*
> *And lost their lives.*
> *You are now lying in the soil of a friendly country.*
> *Therefore rest in peace.*
> *There is no difference between the Johnnies*
> *And the Mehmets to us where they lie side by side*
> *Here in this country of ours.*
> *You, the mothers,*
> *Who sent their sons from far away countries*
> *Wipe away your tears,*
> *Your sons are now lying in our bosom*
> *And are in peace*
> *After having lost their lives on this land they have*
> *Become our sons as well.*

As a great friend of mine from the First World War, who died recently in his nineties, once said to me, "Don't forget - and wear those ribbons proudly for only once a year, for no one can take them away from you; but do so with both pride and humility."

The second letter I was from Monash University School of Psychiatric Nursing, and it said:

> *I am writing to thank you for your assistance in conducting the lecture session on schizophrenia for our*

> *Second-Year students of Psychiatric Nursing. Your expertise has greatly enhanced our students' learning and we very much appreciate the time you have given us.*

It's amazing how a simple letter helped me realise that in the fifty years since leaving school, I had moved from being somebody who feared the future when study seemed so difficult, to somebody who received from college and university such words of thanks.

Again, I received another letter recently, which said:

> *Thank you so much for your services to this parish and again thank you for your beautiful sermons and guidance you gave us. It was so lovely to be told that we are people of importance, God's inheritance, and that eternal life and all that is good is our future. So often we have been called miserable sinners and one has left the church and gone away wondering if there is any hope. Thank you Laurie, you gave us more than hope, you gave us certainty of the love of God, the Joy in Jesus Christ and the fellowship of the Holy Spirit.*

I think this is one of the loveliest and most stirring letters I have ever received. Remembering these letters and my visit to Sheviock I wondered if there might be somebody out there who would be interested to hear of 'my extraordinary life'. Perhaps if I was to be brutally honest, as time closes in, I had a sudden realisation that I was proud of my simple and now contented life.

If I were to write my story it would not be for a broader audience, it would be for me. As I imagined the many hours it would take, recalling and making notes, an inner peace grew, perhaps added by the beautiful spring morning. As I drift back in time – I wonder if I will find solace through writing my story, particularly as my journey is it nearing its end.

Opening my eyes the hypnotic melody of the singing birds is temporarily broken. *If I must put a name to my story*, I think to myself, I would call it *Above and Beyond*. And then with the morning sun bathing upon my face I let myself dream once more.

Having from a young age been sent to this rather exclusive public school, I had been insulated from the hardships and realities facing many of Britain's children of my own age. I had little or no experience of manual work and the lessons of the street were the reserve of others. We relied on being taught to be worldly and tough at school where, and along with our scholastic education, we were prepared both mentally and attitudinally. We were told, and we believed, that we were the leaders of tomorrow. Our physical toughness came from playing rugby and other sports, and being members of the School Army Cadets. We did all sorts of things which would have been considered in those days as very rugged and character building.

But when they call people to the colours, to serve their country in time of war, the armed forces didn't care that you were given privilege - went to a public school and had not known heavy work. There was some kind of belief that as soon as you put on your military uniform, no matter whatever force you went into, you were immediately given the muscle and stamina of a working man. You were expected to have all the skills of those noble people who earned their living by their strength. People such as I, protected, knew none of this; we were at a terrible disadvantage in both endurance and acceptance. I can remember during training when we were being taught to lift a six-inch shell to put into the breech of a gun. There was half a dozen of us who couldn't move the thing, couldn't pick it up. The instructor stood there, jumping up and down, getting red in the face, saliva pouring out of his mouth as he foamed and shouted, "What are you, *@!##*- girls?" utterly disbelieving that this one hundred and twenty-pound, (or was it a hundred-pound?) projectile couldn't be lifted by some of us. Fortunately, there was one man, whose name I have long since forgotten, but he was a bricklayer by trade, who suggested we lift this weight by bending our knees, then straightening our knees, and cradling it in our arms. The instructor, who was supposed to know these things, knew none of the finer points of moving a heavy load. He knew only of brute force and so, with the help of a bricklayer, we learned to stagger across a make-believe gun turret, carrying this projectile in our arms. Thank goodness that people like me never had to do that in the fury of battle, for I am sure we would have dropped the shell and blown all our comrades to pieces.

The forces had a magnificent way also of giving stupid orders, like saying that everybody must "Fall in now." I remember, I think it was Peter Ustinov, on a programme saying how two or three of them, dashing on parade, coming out of a building, got jammed in a door. Like a scene from the Keystone Cops - I saw exactly the same thing happen. Fortunately, I had already gone through the door, but those who followed were either jammed in the door, or couldn't get through the door because of the jam. They were all given punishment of an extra drill for not getting to parade on time; when all they did was carry out the orders. But in haste, in fear of punishment, the common-sense of ordinary people had been lost and they couldn't even manage a door. Once we were to leave the training of make believe and enter the theatre of conflict, haste was not permitted. "Never rush, never panic, if you want to live", we were told; "be controlled and disciplined".

Another challenge I had during basic training was communication, probably not helped again by my public-school voice and ear.

During those early days of training, we were given instructors who, really, no one could understand, well, me at least. I remember doing an elementary gun course where I was told that a certain part of the gun was a "carrier inch pin". Well, I think he said something like a carrier inch pin. When we came to take our exam, a verbal one, of course, because most of us weren't expected to be able to write in those days, I was asked to name this part. I said, "A carrier inch pin, sir."

"How do you spell that?"

"I-N-C-H."

The officer bent over and said, "I think you would pronounce it as hinge, it has an H in front of it!"

When training was over, there was this sudden realisation that there was to be no escaping the war. The bombing raids had brought the hostilities to the very heart of Britain, so you had always been part of the fighting, but it's not the same as knowing that you are about to go into battle. After training, a short leave, then to Naval barracks and, from there, to be drafted to a ship. As we got out of the train after leave, a motley crew we were, piling into the back of a truck. Some old hand was in there, wearing long service stripes on his arm, the salt of the earth, a regular RN man. He said, "Now, Donny, know this, you'll hear those gates bang after yer once you've got in RNB (Royal Naval Barracks) and", he said, "once the doors click, give up all hope of those who have entered therein." And with that great sense of trepidation, you entered the barracks, and listened as clang! went the gate. I realised that this new kind of prison life had begun.

As I remember the War, I can't help but consider how ill-prepared we were to be sent out - to do the duties of combat. The British commanders of the First World War were notorious, but unfortunately, very often, for all the wrong reasons. In the early days of the Second World War, those in charge of us, although they wore an enormous amount of gold braid, said and did things which would make them seem almost idiotic today. On reflection, I think the mistakes and the dreadful trench warfare of World War One weighed heavily in the memory of British people, its commanders and soldiers. As Britain entered World War Two I do wonder sometimes how we managed to win.

With an interest in psychology gained long after the fighting, I ponder whether we should have been trained in mind for what we were to experience; but then again, we were barely trained in the art of war, let alone on how to recover from it.

It's funny how different thoughts – as they flow back into consciousness, trigger different memories. Where did my story really begin? Thinking of psychology - I find myself once more drawn to my school days, for it was there the secrets began.

Chapter Four
The Fifth Column

As the storm clouds of conflict grew over Europe and eventually erupted into war, suspicion of those who were 'different', a fear of sympathisers, collaborators and spies, became apparent if not encouraged. In those times of uncertainty, repressed or forgotten fears, often born from previous military or political encounters resurfaced. Although Britain was not the multicultural country that it is now, it had at one time or the other been at war with most of Europe and Ireland and many people from those places lived within its borders. There was also at the time, a rising discontent particularly within the industrial sector, fuelled by crippling economics and the social and political unrest. In Germany, those same factors had help create the environment which allowed for the rise of Hitler. Britain was then, an unsettled country, and with World War One not yet a distant memory, there was a lot to be suspicious of, both from without and within.

In these more recent times, particularly after 9/11, the attack on the Twin Towers in New York, we are fearful of terrorists. Home grown terrorists have fuelled a suspicion of those with different cultural or religious beliefs, even in those who may be our neighbours and friends. That uncertainty, to be alert but not alarmed, is not in itself a bad thing as we all want to live safety and harmoniously. Unfortunately, history is filled with examples of our susceptibility to having those fears and differences exploited. Today, just as in World War Two, one of the primary defences was 'intelligence'.

With war on the horizon, Britain like a hunted animal, moved to a collective psychology of survival - heightened awareness and suspicion. There were those who sought appeasement and those who wanted to fight, but common amongst us all, was silence and keeping one's counsel. Posters were prominently displayed with the slogan "Careless talk costs lives - You never know who's listening". It would come then as no surprise, although very few people would know, that a gentleman came to our school to talk to members of the Cadet Force, the OTC, as it was called in those days. "Eyes and ears were everywhere", he said.

When the talk was over, I remember asking him a few questions and, as I was about to leave he said, "Do you mind staying behind?" I and one other, whom I don't remember, although I would love to have contact with him if he were still living, stayed and the gentleman asked some things like. "Have you ever thought that we depend upon information given to us by members of the public?" He was right. Where else could the information come from except from the public?

He went on to say, although the order of things I can't remember. "Have you ever heard any sort of rumours? There's a new kind of fighter, a new kind of bomber, or that we have this machine, or that machine? If enemy bombs start to fall you may hear from people that this building or that building was destroyed, this is the sort of thing we would like to know."

"Maybe you will hear of tragedies, or about weapons people think we have, or perhaps don't have. We would love to hear of this. If we know these things, it will help us scotch any unnecessary rumours".

There was a short break in the conversation, a time of silence, which was filled by a young mind processing what he was saying, or what we thought he was saying. And then it became totally clear what was being asked. He said, "Have you ever thought of working for your country? We would love it if you are willing, as it were, to work for us." Again, a slight pause before he went on. "We would like you to giving us these or other pieces of information you think we may find interesting, providing of course that you promise never to tell anybody that we asked you to help us."

He then started talking about some secrecy stuff, the need for confidentiality we would call it today - but mainly I think he said *"secrecy"* to give the role a sense of added importance and enticement. At the time my mind was filled with too many other thoughts to recall the conversation or to truly comprehend what he was saying.

I agreed, but didn't know whether my classmate did or not, which I suppose was the point. I remember thinking *"This is great!"* It seemed wonderful at the time to have a secret that you couldn't share with anybody and to feel part of the war. I don't think I realised it at that time, but what he really wanted was to tap into the leaking of potentially secret information. There must have been any number of people who knew all sorts of things, and who inadvertently, or perhaps in rare cases, purposely shared what was, at the time, secret. Maybe it was as simple as somebody working in a factory who said, "Have you seen our new fighter? We are fitting twelve machine guns, not eight like the old ones!" I guess the better the information, the easier it would have been to trace where the leak came from.

In hindsight, I am sure most of the information I had would have given was completely useless. But at the time, as a teenager in an atmosphere of war, I found the secrecy intriguing and exciting - I wanted to be part of it. With the benefit of hindsight and age you can understand why, in those police states, they entice the youth to be informers. But this was Britain. I was not an informant; I was Rudyard Kipling's Kim serving King and Country.

We were told, my friend and I, before I agreed to be eyes and ears, that there would be no records kept of who was gathering information. To help insure our silence we were told, even if we decided to tell people that we had been asked or said we were doing this, it would be denied. For extra emphasis, he added, even if we spoke of it in a hundred years time it would be denied. "People will think you are lying", he said. Well, it's over sixty years now, and I am sure if people ask me questions, or I was to speak of Z Division, they would deem my answers as purely a figment of my imagination. But I am confident that it would come as no surprise - at that time, people were being asked to listen and report on the things they saw or heard.

Over a relatively short period my involvement changed from just reporting information to being sent places to watch and record my observations. I was told when and with whom I was to meet and give my material. Sometimes, I was instructed to pass my information through the police, Z Division. Looking back, I am not even sure a Z Division existed but the name worked in encouraging me and with the secrecy I was won and enthralled. I was at the time, a willing participant, serving my country before I was old enough to join the forces.

When war finally came and Britain was bombed, the country was bristling with fear and misgivings. There was quite a lot to observe and report. I thought at the time that I was doing the right thing; whether I was or not, I don't know. But I doubt I was the only one.

My own family realised I was out and about doing something and I am sure they thought it puzzling, particularly as I wrote things down, but they never asked. They were to keep their counsel then and throughout the war; and after the war, we all just wanted to forget. My father, having served in World War One, knew and understood my war experience without the need to ask and without the need for me to tell. The bond of a father and son touched by war is a powerful certainty.

In my quest for things to talk about way back in 1940, during the lunch hour at school, I often used to walk a little distance to look for things. I remember one day walking towards the railway line and being awfully surprised to see a train with a steam engine that I didn't often see on that line, stationed just outside Croydon. The train was from the Southern Railway and probably an 'N', or it could have been a 'U' class, which, in those days were uncommon, so it was out of place. It was a very long train with lots and lots of carriages made up of all different types. It was as though the train was comprised of rolling stock, sourced from all over the country. Hanging out of the windows were the scruffiest looking lot of people you have ever seen; dirty, and most of them seemed to be in military uniform. Some were wearing woollen jumpers over their uniforms. As I watched the train, I could only ponder what on earth it was all about. Of course, it was the first of the troops returning from Dunkirk. We didn't know of Dunkirk on that day, but I was to learn of it soon afterwards; a resounding defeat that Churchill somehow turned into a victory, imbuing strength and confidence for the Battle of Britain that was to come.

It wasn't all that long after seeing the train, perhaps a couple of months that an air raid warning went off. It happened during the night and I can still remember the sound of the droning plane overhead. It seemed to go around and round for a mighty long time. I don't remember the exact date. I went outside and looked up, and there, caught in searchlights, was the complete silhouette of the wings of a Heinkel 111, as clear as anything. The bomber didn't alter course. It didn't do anything; it was just flying around in those searchlight beams. Of course, no anti-aircraft guns fired into the sky because, at that time, there weren't any guns. But within a few weeks, the daylight air raids began, and with them, one of the largest and most sustained aerial bombing campaigns in history. One of my most vivid memories of that battle would be in August 1940. I think I remember the date as the 15th of August and, standing on a hill overlooking Croydon, I watched as planes flew in and dived down. Objects fell from underneath the planes, and it looked like two: one under each wing. As these planes dived down, I remember particularly that they made no sound before these great spurts of what looked like water, but was really dust and dirt, rose up hundreds of feet into the air, signifying the bombs' explosion. The planes were right over Croydon Airport and were followed by twin-engine aircraft. Everybody was saying they were Stukkas, JU87s and JU88s but I was pretty certain they weren't. I thought they were Me109s and Me110s, being used as bombers. This was the first time I had witnessed a bombing raid. I remembered vividly that as the bombers climbed away having dropped their load, fighters appeared from nowhere. Hurricanes unleashed their fury on the tails of the aircraft, particularly the twin-engine ME110s.

The Battle of Britain had begun. I read an article in a magazine later that said thirteen enemy planes were shot down, mainly Me110s who were jumped by a squadron of Hurricanes which had been patrolling over Dover and flew at speed to Croydon. I can't remember offhand whether it was thirteen pilots that were killed or thirteen planes shot down. Thinking back to that day now, so many years later, I can still feel the emotions that welled within me. As I stood watching the bombs fall, my home and country under attack, the cavalry came, Hurricanes sweeping from the sky in our defence.

As the days passed, the intensity of the battle in the sky above Britain grew. I can remember as vividly as if it were yesterday the crowded skies, plane after plane, anti-aircraft guns going off, and occasionally, a plane being shot down. Standing with a friend of mine right out in the open, we had taken no precautions, to watch as a fighter, a Me109, got hit. I imagine it was from an anti-aircraft shell travelling upwards towards the ranks of bombers, and this fighter, cutting across the sky, must have accidentally run into one of the shells. The wing fell off, the plane dived away, and where it crashed, I am not too certain but the pilot had managed to escape. As the parachute came down, we realised that it was on fire and the poor fellow, hanging underneath, was heading for the ground, forever gaining momentum and speed. Watching a man fall to his death felt totally different to that of watching a plane being shot down. The machine seemed to spare death from the conscience. I believe he was killed on impact somewhere not too far from Shirley Church in Surrey.

I remember another occasion when thick anti-aircraft fire was filling the air. A plane was hit and as it fell from the sky, it recovered. Slowly, with smoke billowing, it flew past us at a very low altitude. This time, we had hit one of our own. It was a Spitfire and the whole underneath of a wing was shattered. It appeared to head towards Croydon to land, but I don't know if he made it.

The great air attacks and battles in the skies above Britain that spring and summer of 1940 have been well recorded by so many people, but to stand watching, day after day, and spend hour after hour at night with the bombers flying overhead was a remarkable, if not surreal, experience. For a while, the bombers just seemed to fly over on their way to London and nothing happened to us. We knew of the complete destruction that was occurring in London, but we had, for the most part, been safe. Then one night, sitting in a cupboard under the stairs that was supposed to be the safest place, I remember hearing bombs whistling down, and my father saying, "My goodness," (he would never have said "My God" as he was not a swearing man), "they are going to bomb us." It seems now a casual recollection, huddled in darkness under the stairs. Sometimes there would be hours of silence with not a plane or bomb to be heard, and then other times, the drone of engines and explosions off in the distance. But there was always the ever-present threat, listening to the whistling of bombs falling and exploding nearby. My memory of any fear from being under the stairs is long forgotten, fogged by the events of war yet to come; but the sense of powerlessness, waiting for a bomb to hit or miss, remains strong.

When the aerial bombing and the destruction of London was at its fullest fury, it seemed as though every aircraft in Hitler's Luftwaffe was being thrown against the capital city. I remember seeing enemy bombers flying in close formation and filling the sky, line after line of them, and what appeared to be fighters flying above, going around so they formed a pipeline, a protective layer above. They must have gone around in several layers. Then I recall seeing British fighters above that, diving down the pipe to the bombers below, and the rattle of guns. I remember seeing five enemy aircraft falling away with smoke pouring from them and I could not help but feel a small sense of victory at the sight of their destruction. Despite the bombing and the immense devastation, at times, I got a feeling that we were invincible as I watched Spitfires and Hurricanes in the skies above and listened to the distinctive sounds of our fighters overhead. It was a feeling that I would lose the closer to war I became.

We were constantly being told of enormous numbers of enemy planes that were being shot down, and now that we were beginning to see it, we started to believe it. If you went to High Street, almost every day, you would see an enemy fighter being taken away on an RAF lorry. They usually happened to be one of the special squadron with the yellow nose. Long after the war, we learned that the RAF had only one or two of these yellow-nosed fighters, and it was the job of the crew just to drive them around to convince the civilians that we were winning. I don't know whether we needed this morale booster but I suppose it didn't do us any harm. I presume today, we would call such an act 'spin'.

Quite often, I used to go for a walk up the hill near where we lived. If an air raid hadn't started, you had time to get home between the sirens sounding and the bombs falling. It would take me about ten to fifteen minutes to get home. Sometimes, nothing much would happen, while other times, I got to see the anti-aircraft guns and search lights reaching up into the night, lighting the evening sky. With the sirens wailing, the streets would be empty; even the air raid wardens had taken cover. Nobody was about to blow whistles or shout at you to get to safety. There was stillness in the dark of the evening: no sounds of people, cars, or animals; only a background of sirens and the relentless pounding of anti-aircraft fire made by people unseen.

One time, while returning from my hill with sirens sounding, something strange struck me. Often on my way down the hill, I saw a light flashing down in the gully, which today is covered with houses. The light would make its way towards Mitcham Common. I was standing on Pollards Hill in Norbury, South London. It seemed that whenever the air raid siren sounded, which it always did at a similar time most evenings, I would see this light flashing. On one of these days when the sirens started, instead of taking cover, I made my way down towards it. Not knowing what to expect, I crept cautiously towards the light staying hidden in the darkness of the night. I found a little Morris Minor, and in it, somebody was flashing a torch. I had no idea to whom they were flashing, as there were no planes flying, not even the sound of engines in the distance. I carefully took down the number, which I still have to this day. The incident and number formed part of my next report. Nobody said anything, but the next time the sirens started and I climbed down the hill, there was no flashing light and no Morris Minor.

Towards the latter part of 1940, having spent most of my time in an air raid shelter rather than in the classroom, I left my school and got a job in a factory many miles away in the west of Surrey. One night returning home, the sirens sounded and an air raid was on. My train was held up, so to get home, I decided to journey via London, where I caught an Underground because there were no trains going back to my local station. I was told that if I went via a roundabout route on the Underground, I could probably pick up a train from London Bridge. I found myself on the Central Line Underground, and as we pulled into St. Paul's Station, I saw all the people on the platform sheltering from the air raid above and smelled the putrid air. I got out at St. Paul's, but we weren't allowed to go up to the top, so I got a job giving out refreshments. Yet, the amazing thing was, the trains still came in and out, probably to pump the air around so that we could breathe. The bombs were falling, but the trains kept running! I finally decided to get on one of these trains and make my way to the main line station. I didn't realise, but as I came up from underground, I was to be granted a view of what seemed to be the whole of the city of London ablaze. I stood for what seemed an eternity, just watching the city engulfed and burning. You wondered how anyone could survive.

My time as a civilian, was coming to an end and the Royal Navy was about to become my home. It was not until I joined the Royal Navy and read, and I think signed, a thing called the 'Articles of War', that I remembered 'the gentleman' and our 'secrecy' conversation. I distinctly remember wondering about the 'information I had gathered and if it was to be just a thing of the past. But future events would suggest that it was perhaps not just the game I had assumed - a little more serious than I had ever considered. What had started as a casual acquaintance in the simplicity of youth, an affair if you like, had a habit of resurfacing in the most unlikely of times and places.

It happened first with a Parade and then while being interviewed at HMS *Gosling* for special duties. The conversation would suddenly transverse my extra-curricular activities before the navy. It was then that I began to realise, my boyhood adventures were arguably more than they first seemed. They were to follow me in ways I could have never imagined while at school.

Chapter Five

The Empire

In my mind, as clearly as if it were only yesterday, I picture the time when I joining the Royal Navy. I had been working for a firm as a Rubber Engineer, when along came the documents that said I was being called up for military service. I was not afraid when the papers came because war was everywhere apparent and, remembering the night when I saw London ablaze, I knew I wanted to join the fight. It must have been so different for all those men and women from around the world, those not directly threatened, who decided to join with Britain in its defence and the defence of Europe. We were fighting for our very survival; why did they come? Whatever their reasons, thank goodness, they did.

When I was born, and went to school, it was towards the end of the British Empire, now nothing but a distant memory; a time in history. The last leftover bastions of colonial rule would dwindle and vanish after World War Two. At school, maps still hung from the walls with the red, white and blue of the Union Jack dotting the world. I was educated to be proud of Britain and the Empire did bring and contribute great things to the modern world. However, its history of colonial rule was, at times, as ruthless and cruel as any empire that preceded it. World War One would set in place the catalyst for a political, economic and social transformation. These changes, Brittan's crippled finance following World War One, the end of the sterling as the world reserve currency and Britain's decision to drop the gold standard in 1931, a decision it had to make, were the dying breaths of the world's last great empire. Its decision to enter World War Two would seal the Empire's fate and usher in the era of the 'Super Powers'; a time we are still in.

With the bitter memories, trauma and losses from World War One still harboured by its people and, despite being ill prepared, it was Britain's decision not to accept an armistice with Germany that makes me most proud. How tempting it must have been to accept the offer with its promise of maintaining the British Empire and navy, if only to buy time for the build-up of its military and home defences. With all the bias of a person born toward the end of an era and a public-school Englishman, I believe the British declaration of war against Nazi Germany, on 3rd September 1939 after Germany invaded Poland, was perhaps one of those rare, morally right decisions, made even more so with the discovery of the unspeakable atrocities and genocide of World War Two.

Looking back through experienced eyes, historical decisions are often seen in a different light. But even with the fullness of time, it still seems that a country, which at the time, had little chance of defeating its foe, both military and financially, went to war for the greater good. I am, however, not totally naïve. The remnants of British imperialism would certainly have been part of the then government's perception of the greater good. Sir Winston Churchill was the last of the true imperialists. Although I know little of the politics, I write with confidence that some of his military decisions during the war were to defend the remnants of the old empire rather than the most rapid resolution of the conflict. But despite the truth that may lie deep in politics, even now as a Priest and man of God, there are times when it is morally, and even religiously, right for a country to send its sons and daughters to war and this was one of them. The behaviour however of a county at war and the discourse of the atrocities of the victors is, perhaps, for another time.

When the call-up papers came, I had only a few days leave and then a day to travel to the recruitment centre. I haven't seen much written about the emotions you and your family experience when the call up comes. My memories are of those most mundane of tasks like packing your bag. All the while your mother looks on encouragingly, but with a grim soul, harbouring the memories of war just past that were still fresh and raw in her conscience. She was to say afterwards, that as I packed, it was as though I was going away forever and, for the many who never returned, that was true. The final reality of a son leaving home for war came for my mother when, after my arrival at the training depot, the Navy sent my empty travel case back by post. She said it was just like being sent '*something from the grave.*' It's a strange feeling, packing for war - a mixture of trepidation, eagerness and escape. I think in many ways, at least initially, it's more difficult for those you leave behind. They must cope with the helplessness of the constant unknown - becoming prisoners of time, memories of the last war and the mailman.

My father, a reserved and solemn man, said little as I made my preparations. It was not until after the war that he told of his difficulty watching as I packed those final few items. It was his knowledge and his experience of fighting in World War One - the realities and truth of war - which he hid. He said that he did not want to erode my desire and enthusiasm, feelings he also once held - as I prepared to leave in the defence of my country. He gave me a ten-pound note, a touch and a smile as I left, likely never to return. Ten pounds, equivalent to about one thousand dollars today, was to pay for my trip home, from where ever I was, at war end. I placed that ten pounds in my wallet and it never left me. It became my ticket home, my pass, and a symbol of survival.

I went to the main line station at Paddington on the Great Western railway and changed at a place called Ruabon. From there, I made my way to the naval base at Pwllheli, which was known as HMS *Glendower*. As the train rolled on, we kept picking up people, mostly recruits; everybody was young, nervous and wondering what was going to happen. I remember listening with interest to all the different accents. Most of the people were born in Northeast London, where I too had been born, but they were speaking in a beautiful cockney accent that seemed to come from that area. There were also one or two people from other parts of the country. You must remember that we didn't have the opportunities of travel as we now do, so something as trivial as different accents was a new experience at the time. We were quite a happy group but undoubtedly apprehension wasn't far below the surface.

The compartment had seating for about eight but there must have been at least twelve of us squashed in all going to the same place, HMS *Glendower*. When the train arrived at the station, we all got out and were met by a petty officer who lined us up and just said, "Turn right." He didn't give us any orders, I suppose because we hadn't yet learned to march, except those of us who were in Cadet Forces. We ambled, as it were, up into the barracks of the training camp, which was previously a Butlin's Holiday Camp before the war. My first impression was that there was a corner of the ground, inside the fence, where all sorts of Navy things like buoys and other navigational objects were stored; none of which, at the time, I understood.

Upon entering the barracks, we were met by a very kindly old Lieutenant Commander, unlike the boot camp images of American TV shows we are all now accustom to seeing. My best description of the old Lieutenant Commander is quintessentially British. He spoke to us in a very gentle and pleasant way. He said we could play football and rugby and went through a lengthy list of other games we might enjoy. You could have been mistaken into thinking we were at holiday camp. I suppose there was no need to scare or intimidate us into our military training, as war was real and every where apparent. He then said, "You will enjoy your stay here." We were formed into small groups and allocated huts. I can't remember how many of us were in each hut but I think it was six or eight. After a short time, I set off to meet my new-found friends from the train. When the morning came, we were rounded up and our military life started.

First, we went to the medical officer for jabs. I can't remember the number, but how sore our arms were when we went to collect our uniforms! Over the next couple of days, we had all sorts of assessments and spent some time in the 'chamber' to see or to have confidence that our life-belts worked. If you were not a good swimmer or a non-swimmer, the chamber was rather a frightening experience because it was where they used the Davy Escape Apparatus. The Davy Escape Apparatus was a combination breathing/buoyancy bag and the chamber is where they used to train people to escape from submarines, so we were in deep water. I was not too perturbed by the training exercise, except that I suddenly realised I was amongst lots of people with no bathing costumes provided, all stripped in the nuddy, other than a life jacket. In those days, we were probably far more modest than people are today.

I am not going to spend much time reflecting on the period of the training camp. I was lucky, however, for on the second day, I was called to the office where an officer told me that I had been appointed Team Leader of my group. A band was put on my arm with an anchor painted on to show my new status. In truth, being the team leader can be rather an unenviable job. It's a bit like a lot of trainees going into the Army and being that one who was made the Lance Corporal, or the Leading Aircraftsman if it were the Air Force.

The Team Leader is not a full rank; it was just an armband saying that you temporarily had that job. There are many times you had to, as it were, dish out orders, which were given to you from above, knowing that as soon as you finished your training, you would return to being an ordinary sailor, serving with the very people you were giving orders to. As a Team Leader, you had to adopt a friendly, but assertive way of giving orders. I think I was fortunate because I had a similar role in the Cadets, and had already learned some of the pitfalls, so I found this job quite easy. Our team, with its varied and mixed backgrounds, worked well together. In our training group, but not in my team, however, there was one dreadful person whom we all feared. He somehow used to get drunk. He must have been leaving the barracks and sneaking into town to buy alcohol from somewhere. In his drunken state, he went around threatening and waving a knife at people. No one reported him as that would have been against the unwritten code, but fortunately, one night, he got arrested and that was the last we saw of him.

With our training coming to an end in those last few weeks, we took our tests and drilled the military and maritime skills we had learned. I was informed that I finished top of the gunnery and drill school and second overall for the training class. I felt just a little bit proud of myself. It was not long after that, I was sent for. An officer called me into his room and said, "Have you ever considered joining a team like the commandos?" To be truthful, at that time, I was hoping to be put on an officer-training course. If I were interested, I was invited to come for evening classes down in the gunnery department. Several other trainees were also invited and we all went with some hesitation. That evening, we were taught, or rather introduced to, varying components of war in greater detail like gunnery, weaponry and the beginning of close combat. Close combat was known at that time as unarmed combat. Each night, we continued our special training and when the general draft came for our next depot, we were all sent to gunnery school in Liverpool, our additional training forgotten, or so it seemed.

On arrival at gunnery school, I was again made Class Leader as we began the next stage of our Navy training. I had not long been in Liverpool when I was sent for by the Padre. Why a Padre? To this day, I have no idea.

He said, "I see that you have been set aside for officer training and you have been doing commando training, therefore your course here is going to be slightly different from some of the others."

He even alluded, without specific reference, to my pre-war activities. I was pleased to hear that I would be going to officer training, but as to slightly different training, I waited but nothing strange or different seemed to happen, other than a continuation of evening classes in unarmed combat. The intensity of the general training had now really increased. We did an intense gunnery course, including live-firing and infantry work and all sorts of things you would expect as they prepared us for war. Then, about three or four weeks into the course, some of us, a group from the evening classes at the gunnery department at HMS *Glendower*, were sent off to a ship for a single trip.

I don't know that I can even remember the name of the ship. It was a merchant ship which didn't seem strange because we were being trained also as DEMS (Defensively Equipped Merchant Ship) gunners. Upon arrival on board the vessel we were issued or deployed to a gun. From memory, the ship carried a four-inch gun and, I think, a few machine guns: Lewises and Marlins.

Leaving Liverpool, the ship set off for a run to Northern Ireland in convoy with some other vessels. On the way, an enemy aircraft flew over and had a look at the convoy. We exchanged machine gunfire but no bombs were dropped. They machine gunned down and we fired up, but nothing came near us and nothing came down. This was though, my first enemy engagement of the war - the first time I shot in anger and the first time someone had shot at me. It was not like the London bombings, where I was a helpless observer, sometimes watching and sometimes hiding under the stairs. This time, I was fighting back. That first engagement was, at the time, quite exciting. I was part of a fighting force and it was all a little surreal and easy - but the truth, the reality of war was still hidden from me at that time. I was both young and naïve, keen to enjoy my first time at sea. Our small, coastal steamer went to Belfast, where we picked up the important war cargo of turkeys for Christmas dinners. It must have been getting near the holidays.

After this single trip, we returned to our training depot and completed our course. I was assigned to become a Seaman Gunner, to go to the varying merchant ships. Before I left the gunnery school however, I was suddenly taken out of that course and given a 'draft chit' to go to the Royal Naval Barracks, Portsmouth.

For the trip to Portsmouth I was put in charge of somebody who failed the gunnery course. I have already told of the gates that clanged behind us as we entered the Royal Naval Barracks. The Portsmouth training was much broader than gunnery school and I believed they were preparing me for the move to officer training. The course covered things like navigation and signals: Morse and Flash. You can imagine my disappointment and foreboding then, when along came a draft. My first real deployment of the war was to be on the flagship escorting the convoys to Russian. Or so rumour had it when I showed my friends the name of the ship on which I was to be stationed. No officer's course and no commandos for me, just the Arctic convoys, perhaps the thing I feared the most. We had all heard stories from the Arctic convoys. The massive loss of life and ships, the ever-present danger from planes, submarines and freezing weather. With luck, HMS *Scylla* would be going somewhere else, but after another chat with the Padre, I knew that this was not the case and that I was going to Murmansk. I was told to keep studying while onboard the ship for officer's entry upon my return.

Chapter Six

Murmansk

It was now early in 1943, during the mists of winter as we set off for this famous cruiser, which we were to pick up in Newcastle. On arrival to HMS *Scylla*, I remember seeing what appeared to be a monster of a ship, even though it was just over six thousand, eight hundred and fifty tons. The ship looked like it was covered with ants, all dressed in overalls, loading ammunition and stores, all the while working at a feverish rate. Within a few minutes, I was signed in and told to get into my overalls. I was about to lug the heaviest weights I'd ever put on my shoulder. I was a slight man and not that tall and, having never trained for heavy lifting or moving, I knew after that, if I survived the war, I would seek a career that didn't involve such heavy manual labour. It only took a day before all the new recruits had settled in and were part of the routine of the ship. I was put into the forward mess-deck, where I was soon to learn how unpleasant sleeping in a hammock amongst so many tightly-packed smelly sailors can be. The cramped conditions, the cold and the sea sickness only added to the health risks, complimented by the persistent fear of torpedos and the knowledge there would be little chance of escape for those below deck.

We had only been aboard the *Scylla* for a couple of days when the ship was due to leave. The weather was awful - biting cold, or so I thought. The wind was howling and several of us newcomers were doing some cleaning around the deck when one of the officers said, "Well, don't look so cold. It's probably nowhere near as cold as where you will be going!"

I remember saying, "Russia," and he said, "I think you're right."

Although I already knew of our destination and been sworn to secrecy, my heart still sank the moment the words were spoken. A trip to Russia was dangerous and the conditions were purported to be dreadful. If I were still being considered for an Officer Cadet, or CW candidate - I was only supposed to be on board a ship for a comparatively short time. But this ship was not going on a short trip. It was going on a very long voyage – half way out into the Atlantic and then up to Loch Ewe in Scotland to pick up another convoy before gathering with the convoys up in Scapa Flow. It was then to Iceland and finally Murmansk, Russia. As I think back now of the convoys, I remember what someone else eloquently wrote:

> *As long as men write about the dangers of the seas and the heroic deeds of those who take their ships into battle against long odds, they will tell tales of the Murmansk Run in World War II, when merchant ships and their escorts steamed into the stormy Arctic with supplies for the Russian Front.*

Of all the memories, I have of the war, even the events that were yet to come, it was the conditions on board the ship which have stayed with me. Perhaps it was because *HMS Scylla* was my first real deployment and that the experience was so different from the life I had lived to that point. I don't fully understand. But the events of the convoy were burned deeply into my unconscious. Even today they seem unbelievable and despite it being a warm spring morning, I shiver as the recollections of the cold comes creeping to the surface.

It is the one unrelenting truth that remains forever in your conscious memory, the vestiges of an intense, extremely bitter and biting cold. A cold that is difficult, if not impossible to explain, except for those who have been there. I had to wear my best overcoat in the sub-zero temperatures because we had no protective clothing. It wasn't until we had been at sea for what seemed many weeks that they provided us with some kind of warm clothing. Whatever protective clothing they did provide was not enough to go around. The people going off watch on the upper deck used to shed their top clothing and leave it for the next person. The clothing like its sailors, belonged to the ship and not to an individual. Britain must have been in a bad state in the early 1940s, when warm clothing was not even available for its sailors.

The duties on the upper deck lasted for short periods because as we got further north, the cold became even more intense. We couldn't be on duty in those conditions for very long, but the Captain seemed somehow to manage it. He was always there on the bridge, probably because he had warmer clothing than some of us; but mainly I think, because he was the Captain.

Despite the severe conditions and the bitter cold, at times you couldn't help but marvel at the sheer beauty of the Arctic. It must be one of the great natural wonders of the world. I remember one time steaming into a fjord in Iceland. There was this towering mountain, all glistening with ice and snow. I could see in the distance a very small ship, or what appeared to be a small ship. The height of the mountains and the vastness of the fjord distorted your perception. As we approached the ship, it turned out to be the forty-four thousand, four hundred and sixty-ton battleship HMS *King George V*. Although it was seven hundred and forty-five feet long, it was but a mere speck. To this very day, I remember thinking – *this is the truth of us.* A mere speck in space and time. Looking out, I felt our insignificance. It was long after the war when the circumstances of the Cuban missile crisis lead me to recall that day sailing into that fjord. Reading the paper, I was drawn to that feeling of insignificance – or was it now helplessness. We as a people, when summoned together were capable of amazing greatness, yet we had proved time and time again capable of evil in equal quantities. Unlike that time sailing in the Artic, with the advent of nuclear weapons I felt we were now capable of destroying nature itself. But in old age I know that's not true. We can destroy ourselves, and I fear that one day we will. But nature, although perhaps changed, will continue without us. And we may pass into history just as the dinosaurs before us.

The *King George V* was the screen escort on this convoy - JW53 (as I was to learn later). There were some mighty warships in the group: Cruiser Berwick, Destroyers Eclipse, Fury, Impulsive and many others. I don't recall seeing any Corvettes which seems strange because of my interest in such things. However, I know they must have been there. We were even joined by some Russian destroyers.

I cannot recall the actual number of ships in the convoy, but it must have been close to thirty merchant and thirty warships, stretching as far as the eye could see; an amazing sight, bringing the supplies and lifeblood Russia needed to halt the German advance. If Germany could stop the convoys, Russia would fall or so we believed. Our convoys had an escort of battleships in case we had to fight a surface war but they sailed well away from the merchant ships which were escorted almost entirely by destroyers. The destroyers and we, a commodore ship, (a light cruiser) in the middle of the convoy, seemed to do most of the work, dashing about all over the place, and in constant action.

The early convoys took an enormous toll on human life and the instruments of war. Over a million tons of Allied shipping had been sent to the bottom of the Artic by the end of 1942. It seemed as though men were sacrificed against insurmountable odds for an unachievable task. In June and July 1942, with the German war machine enjoying almost twenty-four hours of light, thirty-five merchant vessels found the depths of the Barents Sea, the greatest Naval disaster in British history. I can't, in words, adequately describe the convoys on which I sailed. I can only wonder at the hardships and grieve for the loss of life for those who sailed on those early trips.

It's hard to believe that just twenty-one years after World War One (1914-1918), where an estimated sixteen million people died, followed by a flu pandemic (1918-1920) which killed another fifty to one hundred million, we would once again cast aside our humanity. To use our wondrous ingenuity, not for the betterment of mankind, but to create new technologies with the sole purpose of seeing who could be the quickest at eliminating the other.

Our trip up to Murmansk was most notable for the extreme bad weather. Once we had grown somewhat accustomed to the cold we became quite happy when we were in blizzard conditions because we were fairly certain that we would not be attacked by aircraft. The sea usually had a very long swell, and again, you felt almost safe because it was very difficult for a submarine to fire torpedoes accurately in such conditions. A nice swell and the submarine would have to be far below periscope level and unable to see their target. But on our trip north nature damaged our ships without any assistance from the German enemy. It was a battle against the elements as much as surviving hostile attacks. The ice was so thick, if not chipped clear, could topple a ship. Just touching the ship's railing would rip away your skin. The waves were so high that they could snap a boat in two. Men worked in the extremes of cold, trying to hold course and keep the convoy together. All the time, the U-boats shadowed - stalking, hunting and waiting for their chance.

This was, except for the quick trip on a merchant vessel, my first time at sea. Despite the might of our warships and the convoy escort, you felt inconsequential in comparison to the power and authority of nature. Too much time has since passed, but I think we lost only one ship on our run to Murmansk. It was on the return journey where I was to see my first real hostilities, the harshness of war and the loss of too many lives. I remember nearing home, rushing off to engage what we thought was a German battleship, knowing we would be slaughtered while trying to protect the convoy. And the feeling of relief when the battleship turned out to be two oil tankers.

Murmansk is a port city at the extreme northwest of Russia, located in Kola Bay, an inlet of the Barents Sea. Murmansk lies in the Arctic Circle and was the Russian link to the western world in World War Two. Murmansk and Kola Bay would, during the Cold War, become famous as the base of the Northern Fleet and particularly, its submarines. However, during the war, it was bombed and suffered extensive damage, second only to Leningrad. I had only a short time in Murmansk and was surprised at finding an empty and desolate wasteland where our presence was marginally accepted, tolerated, but not welcome. The convoys were not, I think, seen by the Russian people as we saw them. It was not until after the war, when I was to learn of the magnitude of loss and suffering in Russia, that our reception in Murmansk made some sense. This knowledge cemented an affinity for the Russian people - brought about though the bonds of war.

Docking in Murmansk I had been granted leave to go on shore. In the drabness of what was left of the city, I followed the instructions given to me by the Padres before leaving Portsmouth. I made my way to a more *fashionable house* which had survived the bombing. It stood out within the bleakness of Murmansk. In the rear was a secret brothel, but I was not there for the girls of the night. The Padre had instructed me to meet someone. A person who would make themselves known. No other information had been given. At the time, I did question the directions, but the Padre had remained mute with his eyes saying *all had been said*.

To my surprise and completely out of character with the sternness of the type of people to whom I sometimes spoke, a young and quite beautiful woman greeted me. After the simple pleasantries of introduction, she escorted me to a private room. She just beckoned with her finger and I followed. Maybe if I had been a man of the world I would have wondered, perhaps dreamt of where I was being taken, but it came as no surprise when we entered a small sparsely furnished office. Having been directed to sit, we settled at opposite ends of the small table in total silence. She maintained my gaze across the emptiness of the table that now seemed vast. I can still see that engaging, even alluring and seductive smile. A sweet fragrance of perfume spoke in stark contrast to the stench of the ship. As we sat in the stillness, I secretly fought an overwhelming compulsion to say something. A need to fill the void. With nothing to say and feeling most uncomfortable, I just waited. Blinking but always looking straight into her eyes, the minutes passed as if they were an eternity. Still the silence lingered, but then it began fall away. I became aware of cacophony of sounds and voices from outside the room. As I concentrated, the discordant noise organized itself into the clarity of speech. Finally, and without warning my companion stood, wished me a safe return to Britain and left. For a moment, I remained in my place at the table wondering if something else was to happen. After a short time, I stood and made my own way out of the den of vice. It was clear that my acquaintance with this woman was over. Upon my return to England, never was I to be asked about this meeting, not even when I met the Padre. Like many things, this made no sense.

If I were to write my story, I don't think I would want to tell yet another account of actions on the Russian Convoys. They have been written by people far more expressive in language and pen than me. But I am drawn to the return trip from Murmansk as it was my baptism into the horrors of war.

Perhaps it's the sound made by a fly's buzzing nearby that takes me back to one moment in time on the convoy. I was standing on the bridge during action stations, not long after a German U-boat had sunk one of our freighters and damaged another. I was a lookout for aircraft recognition, but I had, at that time, no particular duty, as I had already identified the Heinkel HE111s that were upon us. So, I had nothing to do but watch as these planes, like a swarm of mosquitos, making shallow dives to release their bombs. As a passive observer, my thoughts were drawn to those times under the stairs, listening to the whistle of falling bombs. I watched as bombs crashed around our ship but more often they were nearer the merchant freighters. The noise of the covering gun and the anti-aircraft fire was deafening. The amount of firepower that the convoy could pump into the air was astounding. Occasionally, you would see a plane peel out of line and, with smoke pouring from it, crash somewhere into the sea.

Standing on the bridge, watching in bewilderment, I must have seemed dazed as the Admiral turned to me and said, "Do you smoke?"

I said, "No," to which he replied,

"You do now" and handed me my first cigarette. So great was the covering fire, I don't think we lost a ship in that attack.

Other times, as if for no reason - from out of nowhere came a deafening crunch and then an explosion. You would think, *"Where did that one come from? Was it a torpedo from an aircraft? Or was it a torpedo from a submarine?"* Then one of the merchant freighters would begin billowing smoke and fire. You could only stand helplessly by and watch as another ship sank, going ablaze to its grave in the freezing water.

It was a difficult sight watching death make its untimely, slow and often agonising call on the people and vessels around you.

Before we left the base in Scapa Flow, Scotland, there was a voluntary church parade and very few people out of the whole of the crew turned up. After battling our way through the terrible weather conditions, the fierce fighting day and night, when we arrived in Murmansk, there was another voluntary church parade. It had to be held in two sessions to cater for all the five hundred people who wanted to attend. Perhaps it was the knowledge they would have to return on the same route from whence they came. Such was the effect on the members of the crew that they felt they needed something spiritual to sustain them. And I was one of them.

After my first real air attack, action stations on the bridge took on a new light. As I have said, my daylight job was aircraft recognition and, as any aircraft you saw was an enemy, there was nothing to do except stand back and become a detached observer. I can still visualise the scene and my accompanying thoughts. I would say to myself, *"I wonder what it's like at Victoria Station? Are the people still getting on the trains, going to the suburbs to go to their homes? And here we are out here, enduring all this. Life can change so much in a year."*

Quite often, our ship would speed away at a heady pace to meet aircraft way out on the screen - as it was called - on the horizon. The sky was nearly always overcast so the planes would come down very low to spot us. Perhaps we would lay a barrage of anti-aircraft fire into the air. We could throw up an enormous amount of covering fire into the path of incoming planes, yet in the most part they just kept on coming. To us they seemed unstoppable, but I imagine to them, we appeared impenetrable. We would then turn and head back at high speed to the convoy, to lay our barrier of anti-aircraft fire over the top of them.

I got to see many interesting things, including mistakes from my vantage point on the bridge. Once I remember watching as one of our destroyers was firing its automatic weapons at a plane diving on the convoy. The anti-aircraft gunners continued following and firing on the plane until it was nearly level with the sea and, in so doing, covered one of our merchant ships with anti-aircraft fire. It must have caused any number of casualties and inflicted some significant damage. It would be a fearful thing to realise that one of your own ships was firing upon you, even if quite accidentally. 'Friendly fire,' I think they now call it. As for the members of our crew, I never remember seeing any panic whatsoever. In fact, everybody went about their duties in a calm and orderly way and was quite different from the scenes you often see in films made about the war. This sense of *calmness of duty* was to remain with me throughout the conflict of World War Two. Indeed, it continued after the war when some of us went onto the minesweeping duties.

My day job was on the bridge identifying aircraft, but my night action station was totally different. It was at the very base of the ship, in the lower steering conning tower (aft steering compartment). A helmsman positioned in the aft steering compartment could carry out steering orders, should the bridge control signal fail. I had the two extremes, the bridge which was at the centre of everything that was happening and the lonely depths, perhaps the most isolated place on board the ship. I think being in the aft steering compartment gave me some insight into the claustrophobic feelings sailors must have felt when locked into the small confines of a submarine. Like a submarine, escape was unlikely, impossible if your vessel was hit. This vulnerability did resonate on your first visit to the compartment when the water tight doors were shut behind you. But the trepidation was quickly replaced by the cold and boredom of war which could last for days, hours, minutes or seconds. You never knew which.

For all those who were below deck and couldn't see what was going on up above, there was during times of action, a running commentary over the PA system made by one of the officers. They were pretty good at it. As unlikely as it may sound, it gave us confidence as the battle raged. I suppose it put us right into the picture - making us feel part of the action. Knowing what was happening around you helped, but was not as good as being on the bridge itself. But even so, it was unsettling to hear over the loud hailer that destroyers on the screen were about to drop depth charges, then you'd hear this Whom! Whom! Whom! When I was on duty, below the water level in my cell, the watertight conning tower, and the depth charges went off, it sounded as though before the Whom! of the explosion, there was a sound like a hammer hitting against a metallic object: Clunk, Whom! It must have been the shock wave from the actual explosion hitting the ship before the sound arrived. Occasionally, when below the deck, there was a different sound, a much more crunching sound. That usually meant that a torpedo had found its target and one of the ships of the convoy had been hit.

Nights on board ship could be very long, not only because it became dark so early, but we were so tired. We were even inclined to go to sleep even when we were on duty. Perhaps that was the only advantage of being locked in the aft-steering compartment – nobody knew if you nodded off. The enduring fatigue of being at sea is something you don't forget. I think we were all asleep with our eyes open much of the time, even while standing.

I remember being on the bridge and was surprised one day to see that we were almost alongside an aircraft carrier, HMS *Dasher*. *Dasher* was known as Woolworth carrier because it was a cheap type, a converted banana carrying merchant ship with a flat top put on it. British engineering at its finest. The suggestion of a converted banana carrier being used as an aircraft carrier would be funny - a humorous joke if it were not true. We sailed slowly alongside the *Dasher* before moving on. Later in the day, we heard that it was lost. I often wonder whether, at that moment, it had already been hit and was in danger of sinking. As I was just an ordinary sailor, I have no idea why we pulled alongside and would not have been told anything unless there was a rescue job or another task to be done. It was much later that I learned the death toll was three hundred and seventy-nine out of the five hundred and twenty-eight crewmen. Many escaped the ship, but died of hypothermia and burns suffered when leaking fuel ignited on the water. Most of the dead were buried at Ardrossan or Greenock in Scotland.

There were seventy-eight Arctic convoys that carried four million tons of supplies, food and munitions to our Russian allies. This contributed hugely to the Red Army's ability to defeat the Wehrmacht. Many of the original convoy records are now lost to time, and with them, an accurate account of individual convoys, the ships and losses. I read somewhere that eighty-five merchant ships and sixteen Royal Navy vessels were sunk by the Germans in the battle of the Arctic. It is the awful weather conditions, along with the dreadful loss of life that is remembered when we recall the convoys.

The Russians acknowledged the bravery of those who sailed, fought and died in the convoys by the issuing of the commemorative '40 Years of Victory Medal in the Great Patriotic War of 1941-45' to allied service personnel. The Russians offered recognition to allied service personnel ten years prior, with their '30 Years of Victory Medal', but it was, at the time, declined by the British government. Not until 2013 and after my death would the British recognise those who served in the convoy with the issuing of 'The Arctic Star', a little late and long overdue.

> Ed Offley – Turning of the Tide.

> *The Battle of the Atlantic was the longest and deadliest naval conflict in world history, and the crucial naval battle of the Second World War. For the British, starved by a protracted war with Germany and almost entirely dependent on supplies being rushed in by Allied ships, the Battle of the Atlantic was a last-ditch struggle for survival. For the Germans and their enemies across the Atlantic, the battle had more far-ranging significance. If the Allies could sustain the British war effort for long enough to assemble an invading force in the British Isles, they could carry the fight into the European continent and, eventually, to Germany itself. But if the U-boats won, Germany would thwart the Allied invasion, strangle the British economy, and force the United Kingdom out of the war.'*

HMS *Dasher*

Top: HMS *Scylla*: Photograph courtesy of the Imperial War Museums London

Bottom: HMS *King George V*: Photograph courtesy Maritime Quest

Chapter Seven

Step Short

On returning to the United Kingdom, and within a matter of days, I was sent back to Portsmouth to report for officer training. I have never forgotten and never will forget that first question I was asked when going before the panel. "How much study did you do onboard the ship?" One must admit, virtually none.

"How much work did you do with the schoolmaster?"

"None Sir." As far as I knew, the *Scylla* didn't even carry a schoolmaster. The convoy had been action, action, action but this was not to be in my favour. In fact, I think the convoy went against me. With less than a week at the Officer Training depot, I, along with several other people, were told that we were being sent on long leave, 'indefinite leave from officer training' it was called. We were sent back to our homes and my officer training days were over before they really began. Before I left I did meet once more with the Padre, but not a word was spoken of Murmansk or the task he had given me. It all seemed a little surreal – perhaps it never happened!

Within a short time, those of us who had failed officer training were called back to the barracks and interviewed as to what we wished to do with the remainder of our training time. What course or path we wished to take. Considering the times, this was a generous offer. We were given a choice.

We were each interviewed individually by a nice, three-ring Commander. From speaking to the others, he said to each of us,

"As you have been on the officer training program, we want to use some of the skills and knowledge you have gained."

He then proceeded to give two options that we might consider. One of the interesting jobs was to become an instructor, another a coxswain on a motor torpedo boat.

I said, "Both of those sound very interesting," while secretly harbouring the desire to be back at sea and part of the war.

It was then to my surprise that the Commander said: "I see you were chosen for commando training at one particular time. How would you like to do all three, commando, coxswain and instructing?" Then after a short pause, the Commander suggested if not directed, that I do the course to become an instructor. We would talk again - about some important duties, if I was successful in completing the instructor's course he said. In the meantime, I was to keep my counsel and talk to no one of our discussions. For a second time an officer implied that I was going to be involved in 'something'. Although nothing had eventuated before, this time I left the meeting with a real sense that something was about to happen and that my life was about to be different. But I had thought that last time as well. But being young the past disappointments were immediately forgotten. I was eager to do well, believing I was about to be involved in something special and so attacked the instructor's course with vigour.

The instructors training was a real step up from my initial training. A very intensive course on instructional technique, parade ground work and all the things necessary for an instructor of new entries into the Navy. The course took about eight weeks. It was a great time of discipline and learning. I really felt that, with all the other training I'd had, I indeed was quite well versed in many things to do with the Navy. During the training, we participated in public parades to coincide with special community activities and events. There was 'Wings for Victory' week and some other special weeks all aimed at raising money for the war effort. We were a very smart drill squad and enjoyed going to these towns and marching through them, looking most official and proud of our uniforms.

At the end of the instructor training, those of us who had successfully completed the course were given our new rank: Leading Seaman. During peace time coming through the ranks, can take up to seven years to achieve the rank of Leading Seaman. In war time, it took only nine months. Of course, we could not have had anything like the experience that the regular Royal Navy Leading Seamen had, but come the morning, we had sewn our badges on and we were out on parade.

Now, the usual scene for morning parade at the Royal Naval Barracks, Portsmouth was for the whole camp to be drilled on the parade ground before the division. The Royal Marine Band then came in, leading the special guard of the week onto the parade ground and we, the newly made Leading Seaman instructors, were the special guard of the week. The practice was for the special guard to enter the parade ground to marching music. The Marine band would then break into the tune of the hymn that was about to be sung by the division, and we had to continue marching to our place on the ground at one hundred and twenty beats per minutes and a thirty-inch step.

We had this enormous fellow as our right marker. He stood a little short of seven feet tall; and he, right through our training, had the horrible habit of allowing his step to get wider and wider, and longer and longer. We would find it very difficult to keep up, particularly if you are somebody like me, barely five foot, seven inches. So as Petty Officer Vesey gave us the instruction for the morning march, he said. "Now when you fall in, the hymn for the day will be 'Onward Christian Soldiers'." His voice became raised and looking in the direction of our marker said, "Step short, the bastard in the front!" If ever you saw me - as a priest in front of the church and somebody said that the hymn is 'Onward Christian Soldiers', it should be no surprise that a wry smile would come across my face. I can still hear those words, *"Step short, the bastard in front!"*

After the graduation parade we returned to the barrack room to find the list of names on the noticeboard accompanied by the various camps to which we, the new instructors, were to be assigned. You can imagine my disappointment when I discovered that my name was missing. At that moment, I completely forgot the conversation before starting the training and marched off and demand to know why my name wasn't on the list. The officer I saw just shrugged his shoulders and dismissed me back to barracks. But it wasn't long before I found myself once again in front of the three-ring Commander.

He said something like, "Ah Biggs, we agreed to have a meeting if you successfully completed the training."

"Well, I am happy to tell you that you are the dux of the class." I had never been called that before in my life. I, apparently, was number one in my marks in nearly every department.

He continued, "Now, what I am going to say to you is confidential."

I was to be sent to the Navy Training establishment in Warrington. The Commander went on to say that there would be three others - whose names would be put up tomorrow, who would also be going to Warrington, and the naval camp there, HMS *Gosling*.

"But," he said. They were going as ordinary instructors. I however, was not going as an ordinary instructor.

"It would be announced," said the Commander, "that you did exceptionally very well in armaments and were top of the school in shooting. Because of that you would do a certain amount of ordinary general instruction work, but also have some additional gunnery duties at one of the other bases at HMS *Gosling*."

"This," he went on to say, "will hide the fact that you will be spending some time away from HMS *Gosling* on other duties." It's hard to recall now but I think HMS *Gosling* consisted of about six separate camps so it would not be difficult to go missing without raising any suspicion.

The Commander was not, as you may put it, apologetic for his vagueness, but did say that all he had been told was that I would be doing some additional military duties along with instructing duties. He believed however that more details would be given to me upon arrival at HMS *Gosling*. And so, with very little idea of what was to really occur, I went to HMS *Gosling 111*, in Lancashire, Great Britain along with the three others.

Upon arrival at HMS *Gosling*, each of us was summoned for an interviewed with an officer. This was standard practice and nothing out of the ordinary. It would be at that interview that your specific duties and responsibilities were given.

When I entered the room for my interview, I was told that three additional gentlemen from the Ministry of Defence were present. In hindsight, I would have said they looked just like the Gestapo or KGB, although I don't think I knew of either of those groups at that time. They were very harsh, severe looking people. It was just a normal interview, very friendly, and conducted by the officer who outlined what my instructor duties would be. I was being assigned to this camp etc., all quite normal and routine things. Then at the end of it, one of the men who looked like they were from the KGB said, "We understand you were a member of Force Z," or I think he said something like that.

I said, "Oh yes," because that was just what you did; I couldn't really say no. *Was he talking about the stuff from school, the convoy, or was it those evening commando classes?* I wasn't sure. I think all these years later, if you wanted something to sound secretive, you just added the letter 'Z'.

He went on to say that the Commander at Royal Naval Barracks had already spoken to me about my additional duties. Well the Commander never said anything about Force Z, or what the special duties would be, but I said, "Yes, he did say I was to have some specialised duties," hoping that more information would be forthcoming while not wanting to appear ignorant.

All these years later it's impossible to recall the exact words of the conversation but I do remember him repeating some of the things the Commander had said. Something like "As you have done very well on armaments and weapons that is the course you will teaching here." And then, "When you take the courses, you will be given a group of about thirty men. At the fifth week of training, the week that is usually given over to some form of cleaning and recreational work, in the middle of the training period for the new entries, you will go with the gunnery instructors to the gunnery course and help in hand grenade throwing, rifle and machine gun firing etc. etc." And that was all he said. I still remember leaving the meeting and thinking, *"There is nothing too unusual about that. Where are these special duties?"* I have never been one to swear, but I do wonder if my recollections have become a little politer with the passing of time.

In hindsight, it was if each person I met believed I understood what was going on. I had not a clue.

Life at HMS *Gosling* happened as they described. At about the fifth week, I went to the gunnery course and returned at the end of my spell. While there I met up with all the other instructors as they came with their trainees for the specific classes we were running. For a while my life settled into a regular pattern, gunnery school then back to armaments and weapons training and then back to the gunnery school. But on about my second rotation, instead of being sent to gunnery school, I was sent to the wilds of the county of Flint. On the banks of the river, Dee. The actual name of the place was Sealand, not all that far from Chester, or the little towns of Shotton and Queensferry. It was there that I finally learned I had been selected for a special squad for secret operations. As part of my induction into the group I was required to sign the Official Secrecy Act. I was to also learn that most of our operations were to be in civilian clothes, which meant we risked being shot as spies if captured. For the next few weeks, which I was to spend supposedly at the gunnery school, I would be away on courses for commando training and motor torpedo boat operations.

I was sent to Fort William, Scotland and the Royal Navy Coastal Forces training base HMS *St Christopher*. The setting for Fort William is striking, on the shores of Loch Linnhe and lying in the shadow of Ben Nevis. It was there that I undertook a very intensive but short course, along with other trainees, for coxswains' duties on board motor torpedo boats or similar type craft.

Having completed my initial training, I came back to Sealand. It was there I was to meet up with some old HMS *Scylla* colleagues from the convoy to Russia. Conversations as they do, naturally progressed to what action you had seen. Although not intended in a malicious way, but I was left with the impression that my previous colleagues believed that I was lucky to be spending my time in this place, as an instructor and safe from the realities of war. After Sealand it was back to the main camp just outside Warrington and then I was sent on leave still pondering what my future held.

Chapter Eight
Raid on Cork Harbour

Returning to HMS *Gosling,* after my special training at Fort William, I was to take my third group of trainees. However my time with this group was shorter than the last. I was soon sent back to Flint, near Flint Castle. The River Dee flows through both Wales and England, forming part of the border between the two countries. Flint is a town in Flintshire Wales lying on the estuary of the River Dee.

I have not seen much written about the Royal Navy World War Two activities around the River Dee and, if I were to write my story, I would be determined not to do any research because it would detract from the memories that you carry and hold as true. I can with confidence say this. There were some seriously secret things happing in Flintshire. But then I suppose you could say that of many places in the UK during World War Two. But Flintshire had its own kind of madness.

In the waters of the River Dee and awaiting us was a very fascinating boat. It was one of a type of ship that was converted from a high-speed merchant ship. They have been designed and used to break through the enemy cordon and pick up roller bearings from Sweden. This ship had undergone further modifications for use by an assault group.

We had one or two days to familiarise ourselves with the ship before once again I returned to the gunnery course and then to the main training camp. But things were to be a little different this time. In addition to my normal training duties, upon my return, I was given several people to *look after*. These people only turned up for private evening courses.

I would take my group(s) through some very basic drill work but the real training was in the stripping down and familiarisation of various weapons and later hand to hand combat. At times when I first started giving the evening class, it became apparent that I was the one being taught. Some of the people attending brought with them and taught me about all kinds of American and German weapons. I remember there were even some Italian guns. Our task was to familiarise ourselves with a diversity of weapons. To be able to strip down and handle any gun we were given. I was told that the people leaving the classes must, wherever they were, be able to handle any type of weapon they found. I was to meet again some of the people from my evening training in my new life that that was about to unfold.

It was not long until I was sent back to Flint and to the ship on which we had spent the two days sailing familiarization. This time, there was a group of us, not just a sailing crew, and nearly everybody, albeit ordinary people, was at least the rank of Leading Seaman. In fact, we didn't seem to have anybody ordinary on-board. I remember feeling a little out of my depth. It was at the first briefing when we were told that our duty was as a special assault group. This made me feel even more out of my depth. I was surprised to see that some of the people from my evening gunnery training (varying weapons) classes were among the troops. At the end of the short introduction, we were reminded of the need for the strictest secrecy and that we would spend a little time on the boat familiarising ourselves once more with the vessel before venturing out on our mission, for which no details were given at that time.

For about the next twelve months, this was to become the pattern of my life. Leaving my Instructor duties to participate in clandestine missions and then returning to my instructor duties before being called away once more.

Perhaps if I had been an officer I could recount some of the missions within the context of why and where we were going. I might even know what we hoped to achieve and the code name of the missions, if they had one. But I was just a Leading Seamen following orders. Even to this day, I am not fully aware of what we were doing.

For the people like me who are interested in the various types of ship, our first mission was on a blockade runner. It was originally built by the company, Camper and Nicholson. I believe they weighed about ninety-five tons and were one hundred and seventeen feet long by just over twenty feet wide. They carried three Davy Paxman diesel engines which were supposed to give them a very high speed but in fact they were too heavy and not all that fast. One of them had Packard-built Rolls Royce engines and indeed, could do about thirty knots. Unfortunately, the one we had, with its diesel engines, was lucky to push out more than twenty-four knots. They had some amazing names and I remember such things as *Gay Viking* and *Gay Corsair*. Today, you wouldn't use the word 'gay', particularly on a warship. Most were lost in mercantile use. The one we had, as I said, was converted back to some kind of motor torpedo boat. They were designed to carry forty-five tons of cargo. The idea was that the cargo hold could be used for carrying fuel and, being diesel, they had a long range. It gave us great distance, but unfortunately, they were also rather slow and unreliable.

The briefing at Flint was the first time the whole crew (sailors and assault group) had met, except for some of us who had been part of the first familiarisation trip. Everybody, as I have said, seemed experienced and professional and there was a mixture of ranks. We were, at that first briefing, told who did what and that more details would be given latter. I remember amongst the assault group there was a captain in the Royal Marines. Because we were all new however, it was difficult to know the rank of anybody, as we didn't wear uniforms. At least, we did wear uniforms on this familiarisation trip, but under our protective clothing. For the trip, we sailed down to Pembroke in South Wales and Milford Haven. We had engine trouble on the way and I was given the job of being on the helm for nearly the whole distance.

When we arrived at Milford Haven, the captain of the vessel, who was a Royal Naval lieutenant, informed us (the sailors) that when we went on the covert operation, we would not be told where we were going. We would only be told which people were to oversee the various functions of the boat and the mission. When the actual time to leave came, I was terribly surprised when he turned around and said that onboard the ship there was to be the captain, himself, the first lieutenant, and another officer who was mainly the navigating officer. Then, if it came to anything to do with the movement of the ship, I was next in charge. I had gone from being an ordinary seaman on the Russian convoy to suddenly finding that I was number four on this ship, as far as moving it was concerned. Thinking back, I imagine the idea was that in the event of injury, death or loss - if I were the one that was left, no matter the rank of anybody else, it was my job to get that ship home. Presumably, the training I received in navigation and signals, which did not gain me a commission (officers training), was good enough to take a warship back home. It's amazing as I think about the war – those events so many years ago - that I still harbour resentment at not making it through officers training. It's surprising what strong and powerful emotions recollections can trigger!

As we prepared for what was to be my first mission, the vessel had engine trouble, again. Rather than call off the trip, another vessel was found. What the gap in time was I can't recall. But I do remember being quite surprised when a United States motor torpedo boat arrived. I had never been on this kind of craft before. It was a Higgins-type motor torpedo boat weighing about forty-six tons, seventy-eight feet long, and this craft was fast. It had a top speed of about forty-two knots, four thousand and fifty horsepower to push forty-six tons. Rather frighteningly, they had put extra fuel tanks on the upper deck to give it sufficient range and we had far too many people on board with the assault group. We had two days' familiarisation with the new vessel before being ready for the unknown.

As we left harbour and were heading out to sea, I was given the helm and told of our destination - in case of problems. We were to sail to just off the southern coast of the Irish Free State, as it was then known. In fact, we were going quite close to the entrance of Cork Harbour one of the most beautiful locations in the world and a place to where I would return many times after the war.

The trip, I remember, was long because we went at such a slow speed for a vessel of that type. Barely twenty knots - to conserve fuel I imagine and to ensure we arrived at the right time. It was dark of night when we slowed and finally stopped at our predetermined drop off point. We were now about four nautical miles off the entrance to Cork Harbour - Roches Point and the entrance to one of the world's biggest natural harbours. It's two and a half kilometres long and just one and a half kilometres wide, second only to Sydney, Australia. It became a major shipping port early in the nineteenth century. Great tragedies, such as the Titanic and the Lusitania became associated with the harbour. The Lusitania, on voyage from New York to Liverpool, was torpedoed by a German submarine on the 7th May 1915; she sank within eighteen minutes at the cost of some twelve hundred and one lives, including one hundred and twenty-eight U.S. civilians. The sinking of the Lusitania heightened tensions between the U.S. and Germany and moved the Americans closer to joining the war.

Britain had, until 25th April 1938, maintained Naval bases at Queenstown (Cohn) and Berehaven until Prime Minister Neville Chamberlain handed control of the ports back to the Southern Ireland government. During the First World War, the Naval bases were of significant strategic military importance, being refuelling and staging posts for Royal Navy ships on patrol in the Atlantic protecting convoys. The abandonment of the ports enraged Churchill, who said, "A more feckless act can hardly be imagined for it will be impossible to retake the ports when needed as some members have suggested." The loss of the ports reduced the radius of Atlantic protection by more than four hundred miles, with flotillas having to operate from Pembroke Dock or Falmouth. Even though Ireland remained neutral, the potential that the Free State may have assisted the Germans persisted in the mind of Churchill and didn't help the tension that existed between the Irish and British governments.

In total silence, we made ready the small boats we carried on the upper deck. Each boat was equipped with a rather low-powered outboard engine and oars. We put three of the small boats into the water, one either side of the ship, and one across the bow. The assault team, carrying American weapons and made up of about six men and their equipment, took off to an unknown destination. We didn't wait around; as soon as the small boats were underway, we turned and headed back to Milford Haven. We refuelled and, as tired as anything, snatched a few hours' sleep. We were awoken and then set off again to the same point, the place where we had despatched our assault teams only two days previously.

Under the cover of darkness, we once again neared the entrance to Cork Harbour – perhaps a little closer in this time. Then rather like a scene from B-rated Hollywood film, we waited silently bobbing about in the water, concealed by the night and listening for enemy craft. A flash from a torchlight somewhere closer to shore briefly penetrated the darkness. We acknowledged the signal. A short time later those who departed two days earlier came aboard. Instead of taking the small boats back on board, they were sunk. Holes were punched in their bottoms so they wouldn't float around and would eventually sink. The small boats had the words, *'US Navy'* on them. Presumably, I thought at the time - this was because these Higgins boats had been American PT boats. With the passing of time however, maturity and a better understanding of politics, I doubt whether this was the case. We started our main engines and I turned the boat for home, leaving the half-sunken dinghies in the water.

After a few minutes, there was a flash of light on the horizon and the glow of an explosion. Somebody said, "Three cheers" and on the deck of our boat a muffled cheer went up - we were still sailing in foreign waters.

The words were passed around, "Mission accomplished".

On the return trip, people said very little as we each had our duties to perform. I was to (again) remain on the helm for the entire journey back home to Milford Haven. We (the sailors) were never told of our target and nor was it spoken of on the boat. It seemed to me obvious that we had blown up an oil tanker or perhaps a merchant vessel acting as a refuelling tanker for German U-boats in Cork Harbour. Did I think that at the time, or is that a conclusion I have reached with hindsight? I don't in all honesty know, but there were, both during and after the war, rumours of the free Irish refuelling U-boats in the harbour. As early as September 1939, Churchill said there was evidence of the Irish providing support to U-boats. Since the end of war, however, the rumours have been denied by both the Irish, German and British Governments. In contrast, there appears to be a consensus that the free Irish were not helping the Germans (refuelling submarines) and that Britain did not conduct any raids in free Ireland. Just 'unsubstantiated rumour' is what I read somewhere.

My first clandestine operation then was to deliver operatives to Cork Harbour, blow up a ship and, if anything were found, make everything look as though it was done by the Americans. Of course, the British would never do anything like that and certainly not blame it on their allies. I think the American connection may just have been accident however – although I can't reconcile why the assault group carried US weapons. Our original ship had broken down, and how fortunate that the US ship was available with its fuel tanks already modified for a long journey.

Even today, all these years later, I wonder if our allies would hold anti-British sentiments if they knew the British mounted operations against them. I was sworn to hold my counsel and keep my silence. The Official Secrecy Act for World War Two has long been lifted and one's hope is that in hindsight, after all these years, it would just be seen as a part of war, or as the French would say, "C'est la guerre," (It is the war).

At Milford Haven, we all dispersed back to whence we had all come. I don't know where the others or the boat went. I didn't even know what happened to our converted merchantman – the one we had left behind broken down. I had to catch the train from

Milford Haven back to the camp in Warrington with only my case of clothes. We were required to leave most of our issued equipment behind. That's an interesting thought! When I started thinking about this story, I remember recalling how on the Russian convoy we were so poorly equipped. Not so on this particular journey to Cork. I was issued with the warmest of clothing, the latest in life-belts and a special new type of steel helmet which had no rim. We even had gloves! Everything one may have needed including a new type of gas mask.

It was, as a young man, one of the most difficult tasks in the world, going back to the navy camp outside Warrington and acting as though everything was normal. It seems wrong all these years later, to admit I had a real sense of satisfaction - a 'high' coming back from a successful mission. I remember my father being quite surprised when I came home. Upon my return to Warrington I was sent again on leave. I remember him saying, "Don't you people do any work? You're always on leave!" But I had a bag full of dirty clothing and my mother dutifully washed it for me and, wise lady that she was, said, "You've been to sea." I said, "Ah, yes just a training operation. When we do training, of course, we'd go onboard ship." Mothers, I think, have a sixth sense. I always felt she was not quite satisfied with my answer. But even within families, during the war, you kept your own counsel and when the war was over, we didn't want to speak about it. I was so tremendously tired which again raised my mother's suspicions, but then, I suppose, that was to be a factor of wartime. Constant fatigue and tiredness.

After a short leave, it back again to do some more instructor work. Once again, I was given an evening group for special weapons and combat training. This time the people I was teaching all spoke with overseas accents - some of them French and all stern and standoffish. The training was comparatively short but very intense, particularly the unarmed combat.

It was not long before I was on a train again when supposedly I was going to gunnery school. This time the train was to take me to Cornwall and what would become the headquarters for a number of our operations.

Chapter Nine

Cliff

The headquarters for the next series of special operations was a private house not far from Fowey in Cornwall. The actual place, as far as I know, doesn't show up on any maps. I possess, to this day, a modern ordnance survey map, but the name of the little township is not there. It was quite a decent-sized house in this village, which bore the name of Cliff. Its actual location was near the villages of Lerryn and St. Winnow. There's a fork in the river, which runs down to Fowey and then very deep water. A vessel being tied there would bear no suspicion whatsoever.

Fowey itself was the base for a Coastal Forces flotilla during the early part of the war.

Arriving at Cliff was rather like a reunion, entering the house and meeting most of the colleagues who were on the previous vessel. It sounds a little corny, reflecting for a second on my own thoughts - reunion, meeting friends. How could that be when we had only done one mission and some training together? The tenuousness of life in times of conflict, have I think, a habit of speeding everything up, particularly relationships.

All the officers and crew were there, but none of the people from the assault group, the ones who took part in the actual landing at Cork Harbour. We were added to by, I remember, a rather beautiful brown-eyed lady Wren officer. She seemed to be in charge of the organisation. We also had a new group of passengers.

After arrival, we were kitted out, ate and got settled in to our new surrounds. We were all accommodated in the house and despite rank, were all put in together, that is both officers and men. This was a little unusual for the Royal Navy. I was not a beer drinker, but there was beer and everything you could need. I recall it being a friendly and relaxed group.

Like on our trip back from Ireland, the rules seemed to be that nobody talked about what we did or where we had been, although one of our crew members did say to me. "When you came aboard, I thought you were a new boy. Obviously by your performance on the helm you were anything else but new."

I knew what he was saying was true, I had no experience. I really was a 'new boy'. Just then one of the officers turned and said something like. "Now we don't talk about where we are from or what we are doing, but when you've been to Russia like this man has, then you can start asking questions." That brought silence to the room. It was rather a funny feeling. I still considered myself as raw, yet I had now participated in one secret operation and been to Russia. I wonder when you cease feeling new. Later in life, when I faced those moments of self-doubt, I would recall that moment and use it to push forward. I tried never to dismiss the doubt, for it's the thing that keeps your feet firmly on the ground, but instead sought to treat self-belief and self-doubt as important partners.

The day after our arrival the planning for our next operation began. We received a briefing and some information from the brown-eyed Wren officer and the Commander, albeit limited. We were assigned the respective roles we were to have while on board the ship. Again, I had no idea, at that time, why we were going. Except for one occasion, the whole time I was involved in these types of operation I would never know *WHY*.

Our passengers also arrived sometime after our briefing and unlike our Cork trip, these were not Commandos. They were, if I can describe them as such, of the secretive type, the type I had recently been training in the evenings.

Our converted merchantman was there, the Camper and Nicholson boat that we had abandoned before the last mission. We all hoped (in private) that its Davy Paxman engines would be operating smoothly this time. Despite its dodgy and unreliable engines, the advantage of this vessel was that there would be far more space on board for our passengers and their equipment, unlike our US boat.

Leaving the river Fowey, we set out very quickly and made our way to the Isles of Scilly, where we refuelled. Leaving those islands, we headed across the channel in absolutely dreadful conditions. While heading into the Bay of Biscay, rather frighteningly, we were flown over by an aircraft, which I identified as a Dornier 215. It was flying high and appeared to take no notice of us. The weather became so bad that the trip was called off and we returned without stopping, straight back to Cliff. We arrived back early in the morning. In contrast to our trip it was a clear and beautiful morning. We sailed up the water from Fowey to a little town called Golant, Cliff was on the right. The town of Lerryn was further up the waters and if you went far enough you would come nearly to Lostwithiel, a most beautiful part of the country.

After docking it was back to the house in Cliff where we disposed of our surplus equipment. This time there was no second attempt at the mission. It was, with a travel warrant in my pocket, to the railway station at Lostwithiel and back to Warrington where I was immediately set to work with a new class of sailors still in their first few weeks of training. I remember a different feeling returning to the Warrington mess deck this time. While after the last mission it was something akin to *satisfaction*, this time I looked round and pondered: *"Was I the only one here taking part in these kinds of operations?"* It was not that anything happened on this voyage, it was just a most unpleasant trip to France. It was not until after the war that I learned that there were all sorts of special groups operating, so perhaps I was not alone on the mess deck but who is to know? The other instructors did not question my disappearances, however the trainees were no longer sent to the gunnery range, where, it was said, I went during my absences. By that stage of the war, they had opened a new rifle range very much closer. Trainees from other camps were sent to the Flint area, so it was rumoured that my duties from time to time were in Flint, but of course, I wasn't going to Flint.

I had not long been back at Warrington when I was sent for once again. I went to Camp No. 1, which was headquarters, picked up my gear, caught the train, and once again, I found myself back in the house at Cliff. Like our last mission, the night before we left was quite a party spirit. Following a quick briefing, where once more we were only told of our duties, we all gathered, including our new passengers and set off once again. I presumed that as we had not successfully completed our previous mission, we would be going to the same destination but we most certainly did not go toward the Scilly Isles. Spending most of the time on the bridge and on the wheel, I realised that we were heading in the direction of the Channel Islands. The timing of the trip had been arranged so it would be night as we neared the Channel Isles, off the coast of France. Most of the action undertaken by British Coastal Forces during the Second World War occurred at night for good reason; stealth and avoiding superior enemy firepower. For our types of missions, stealth and evading any enemy observation and contact were essential

We had a very uneventful daylight part of the trip although we did see a few British Typhoon fighters who came quite close. They flew on towards the French coast. Apart from that, we heard and saw nothing. As evening fell and we gained the cover of darkness, we picked up a number of British motor torpedo boats out on a patrol. We passed each other without incident.

By now it was quite late and running silently using the cover of darkness we approached the Channel Isles. Our passengers made their preparation to leave the boat as we were closing in on the Channel Isles. I was instructed to slow and lay off the coast. All these years later I'm not certain which of the islands we were near, or how far we were from Guernsey. Stopped with the motors off our passengers made their final preparations as they prepared to depart and we made our final preparation to go close in shore. But suddenly, WHOOM WHOOM, all hell opened up. Heavy guns started shelling us. Our cover was broken and we were forced to make a hasty withdrawal. It was now impossible to land the people we had on-board, whatever their operation was.

The Channel Islands off the cost of Normandy, France, were occupied by Germany in June 1940. The Islands formed a resistance movement but not on the scale of France. Whether our operatives were to assist the resistance or target battlements I will never know but their equipment gave the impression they were going to make 'A Big Bang.'

Once again, we made our way back to Cliff and, for a second time, were unable to complete our mission. Not long after docking we were dismissed, returning from whence we came, disappearing back to our normal war time duties. Or so I assume, because that is what I did.

I had a number of trips between Cliff and my instructor duties at the gunnery school for advance combat training - in particular hand to hand combat and high speed sea drops and pick-ups. The learnings from Cliff were quickly integrated into my after-hour's classes back at Warrington. It was not long however before I was summoned once again to Cliff for another operation.

Arriving at Cliff, I was met by our brown-eyed Wren officer and my colleagues from the previous operations, now rightfully called my friends. The atmosphere however was different. Our little group, although professional, had on previous occasions been more relaxed. Hierarchy although clear was not overt. And as previously mentioned, the officers and men bunked together. Rank, while worn, was often hidden under other clothing even while onshore. On this occasion as I entered the house, I sensed things were different. There were additional personnel about and rank was clearly on display. The atmosphere was 'formal' and there was not quite so much fraternising with the ranks. The party atmosphere was absent and there was no beer the night before the mission.

Our passengers on this occasion were French who kept very much to themselves. I recognised two of the French operatives, from when I took them for advanced weapon training up in Gosling. They acknowledged me with just the slightest bowing of their heads but not a word was exchanged between us.

For this trip, we had a new and extra crewmember, a petty officer wearing a Petty Officer Coxswain's badge on his arm. As I had performed the coxswain's duties on all previous missions, I thought. *"Oh well, I've lost my job as coxswain on this one"*. Then the nagging self-doubt kicks in and all sorts of thoughts flooded my mind: *"Was I to lose my place in the team? Had I not performed? Was I to be replaced? Then, why had I been summoned? Was I to have a new role?"*

On our previous and perhaps more relaxed gatherings, there was no speaking of the mission outside of the briefing, and no asking of questions of each other. Our new crew member, in those few days of preparing for departure, started asking a lot of questions regarding previous operations, what this operation might be and our duties outside of the team. The day before the mission he was taken out of the team. I never saw him again. So, I was learning - 'See all, hear all, but say nowt.' Perhaps that was the lesson from my visit to the *fashionable house* in Murmansk

Our brown-eyed Wren officer gathered us all together, including our passengers in a room for a briefing. I remember this occasion well because it was the first time the crew and passengers had a briefing together. The other difference was, we were given some quite specific details of the mission.

I recall a solemn briefing. We were told that this time we were going on a very long and dangerous operation with the free French. Our target (drop off) was to be near La Rochelle, right in the middle of the Bay of Biscay. I remember thinking, *"How are we going to get that far on our ship?"* The briefing gained additional purpose when we were informed of the German U-boat operations and pens at Brest and St. Nazaire. They spoke of the underground submarine shelters and their great concrete buildings. It took little imagination, particularly after the 1942 raid on St. Nazaire, to know this would have been one of the most guarded places in the world. Having been on the Atlantic Convoys I knew how valuable intelligence on the U-Boat pens would be.

The actual disbarments destination for our operatives would not be revealed until we were in the Bay of Biscay. It was however to be a harbour and not a sea drop. In the briefing, we were given to understand that there was an enormous amount of coastal shipping coming up from Spain and France. The fishing and merchant vessels were moving along the coast in the Bay of Biscay to La Rochelle, Bordeaux and the neighbouring ports. The plan was, using the cover of bad weather, to make the crossing from England to the Bay of Biscay. Our vessel was carrying a boom or derrick rather like a merchant ship, which indeed we really were. It had had its armaments removed for this trip. The twenty-millimetre Oerlikon had been taken off the bow and the twin Oerlikons were taken off their mounting. Using a superficial disguise as a Spanish merchant vessel, the plan was that we would just simply raise the Spanish flag, sail in to port, tie up, unload our cargo of spies and return home again to England, all while being totally undetected.

Thinking about my story I pause to ponder this mission. I wonder when the *powers that be* came up with this plan – what chances of success were prescribed to this mission. Or is that a more modern phenomenon. A privilege for countries not engaged in all-out war.

As for a plan, it was simple indeed. Since the early days of the war a very small number of converted merchant ships were used as special services vessels and disguised as Spanish or Portuguese freighters. They were often used for landing agents and to pick up escaped prisoners, dangerous missions in themselves, but not this close to major German sea bases. And not since the 1942 raid on St. Nazaire, where the Royal Navy sailed an old destroyer, HMS *Campbeltown*, fifteen motor launches, one motor gunboat and one motor torpedo boat across the Atlantic, into the Bay of Biscay, and up the river to the harbour of St. Nazaire. After the raid on St. Nazaire, Hitler ordered the building of what became known as the Atlantic wall coastal fortifications up and down the coast.

And so, with the knowledge of La Rochelle and our mission in mind, we gathered and boarded our ship. Once again, I was at the wheel as we set off. Although it was unspoken amongst the crew, we all knew that this may very well be a one-way journey.

The plan or at least the first part of it was to use the cover of terrible weather forecast for the next few days. No turning back due to bad weather on this occasion. True to the forecast, as we departed, the weather was utterly appalling.

We set off in daylight and the course, which I was plotting, dropped south as though we were going towards the French coast before turning out towards the Atlantic. The weather was horrific, the waves were breaking over the ship and we took a pounding. The ship was rolling and lurching violently. Forward speed was all but none, and we made little headway. The weather was so ferocious that it was no longer our friend. The decision was made that if we did not seek shelter, we might never cross the Celtic Sea. Too much was at stake to risk the ship being damaged by the sea. With bad weather forecast for the rest of the week, we turned around and went back to the Scilly Isles hoping to wait out the very worst of the storm. After about two days the weather calmed just enough. We set off very early one morning, an eerie mist hung in the air as we left the harbour and once more ventured into the open sea. This time we could make good head speed. The ship had quite a bit of speed in reserve but not wanting to compromise our fuel we maintained a steady twenty knots. Our course was almost due south. We sailed all day and night and then right on into the next day. That following day we sighted an enemy aircraft and reduced the speed to about eight knots. This was to allow the vessel to wallow around - rather like a French fishing boat, or so we hoped. The plane moved on and showed no apparent interest in us. That was not to say however that it had not radioed our position to a German costal patrol.

Although conditions were still quite overcast, a few other aircraft also flew overhead. I am pretty certain that I saw a DC3, which probably meant it was one of those that flew from Gibraltar to Britain. The other aircraft I remember, which I could not see clearly, may have been, with its swept back leading edge of the wing, a Heinkel 111.

With a two-day stop at the Scilly Isles and the considerable distance of this mission, we were by now looking very scruffy. It was impossible to shave in the rough weather and the great long swell of the waves. Things weren't helped if we went between decks because most of the Frenchmen onboard were suffering terribly from the effects of the weather. To say they were seasick does not adequately describe their absolute discomfort. I suddenly realised how lucky I was that I did not suffer from the effects of seasickness, not even when between decks. It is fair to say however, that the smell of other people's vomit, does have a most unsettling effect! The stench remained me of the trip to Russia, a smell that eventually I became accustomed to.

After what seemed a long and difficult voyage weather-wise but luckily uneventful enemy-wise, we turned due east and headed for a place near the river that led to Bordeaux. By now it was night and I was told we would be making landfall very close to a place called Royan. Royan was quite a sizeable town about one hundred kilometres south of La Rochelle with two fortresses defending the Gironde Estuary which led to the Garonne River and the Port of Bordeaux. Although it was not La Rochelle, it was still a very dangerous place. The Port of Bordeaux was known as a major distribution port for the German war effort and the home of more submarine pens. Like St. Nazaire, the British had once targeted shipping in Bordeaux when in December 1942, under the code name of operation Frankton, a detachment of commandos in canoes paddled up the estuary and attack cargo ships moored in the Port of Bordeaux. The Germans were aware of the danger of allied shipping entering the estuary so the area was well defended and patrolled.

The coast line in that part of the world is generally flat, long and uninteresting. We dropped just short of Royan and, unchallenged, sailed right into this very small port, a fishing village which was memorable as it was set under some small cliffs. I don't know the exact location and until this very moment, recalling the story, have never thought of trying to find it.

We were, by now, flying the Spanish flag and believe it or not, we sailed in completely undetected and made a land strike. In the dark and in total silence we disembarked our French passengers. With them safely ashore, we turned the ship around and, still using the cover of night sailed out of the harbour. Once clear of the harbour we dispensed with any pretence of being a wallowing Spanish merchant vessel or French fishing boat. The order was for maximum speed and a bearing of due west until we were eventually clear of occupied waters.

The return journey home was uneventful and, if I recall correctly, even the weather was also reasonably pleasant. Our destination was our home port of Cliff. Having returned return home, we were told that this had been a highly successful operation. Our cargo of agents who originally came from that area, were safely on shore. Of course, nobody said anything about the roles of the agents. One can only assume their job was to spy on the activities around La Rochelle, the principle U-boat depot for the German submarines operating in the North Atlantic area.

From Cliff, it was once more back to the training camp where I spent the last week with one of my former classes. I was then sent on leave before going back to pick up a new lot of trainees.

Life as an instructor was not always as safe as it might otherwise seem. It can be highly dangerous, particularly when you let a bunch of eighteen-year-old trainees, who have never held a weapon before in their lives, loose with guns and explosives. In fact, one of the nearest times I ever came to being blown to pieces was as an instructor. We had taken a new group of entries, who had been in the Navy almost a month, to the rifle and grenade-throwing ranges. There was an old chief petty officer, I think his name was Jimmy James and he was at least seventy years of age. He used to take the base plates off the hand grenades with the trainee watching, replace the fuse, screw up the base and give the grenade to the trainee.

The trainees were then instructed to go to the throwing bay, where I would see that the trainee held the grenade safely in his hand. There would already be another trainee, waiting to throw his grenade, upon the instruction from an officer in a watchtower further back.

He would shout, "Prepare to throw, and in your own time," then "throw." It was always very difficult. You had to make sure that the trainees knew it was the instructor who said when the actual throwing was to happen, and it was in *my own time*, not the trainee's time. The officer was calling to me, the instructor, not the trainee.

The usual drill went something like this: finger into the ring of the grenade, pull the grenade away from the ring and throw the grenade in over-arm fashion. You then got both the trainees to look over the parapet so they could see the smoke coming from the fuse, which was a nine-second fuse. You always prayed that nobody put in a three-second fuse by mistake. You'd hear the officer call from the bay, "Down," when he thought the grenade was smoking enough to know the nine seconds were almost up. That's when you got down. Then BANG! Off the grenade would go and splinters and dirt would fly everywhere. Like a production line, the trainee would move out and another person would enter the bay as the chap who just came in would prepare to throw. It went like this for a considerable time, until all the trainees had passed through.

Well, on this one occasion, I was instructing when another man appeared in the throwing area as one left. I suddenly looked around to see he was holding a smoking grenade. This meant that he already pulled out the pin before entering and the nine-second fuse was running. This small and very nervous young man was clinging onto the smoking grenade as if his life depended on it, although the reverse was true.

I think this was the only time I have ever kneed a man in my life. I kneed him in the place where it hurts the most and, of course, he fell to the ground, letting go of the grenade. I caught the grenade and threw it (not in the approved manner, but like throwing a cricket ball from the boundary) and shouted, "DOWN! DOWN!" and BANG! The thing went off. I wonder how near we were to death. I think about one and a half seconds! So even as an instructor, doing instructor's duties, I think sometimes I was in more danger than the hazardous trip I took near La Rochelle.

After being back at the training camp for a short time, you quickly settle once more, into the daily routine of being an instructor. But before long the next set of marching orders arrived: It's back to the main camp at Warrington to pick up your gear, a train to Lostwithiel and finally Cliff. The usual people and our brown-eyed Wren officer were there. I was surprised when she came in and said,

"Hello Laurie. I'm pleased that we have you back with us again." Then looking down at some papers she was holding added. "Oh yes, it's operation number five for you. My goodness, you are halfway through your stint of duty."

This was the first time I knew that we had to do ten of these things! I suppose now we might call it a tour of duty.

Our brown-eyed Wren officer, was a very friendly soul, quite stunning and a very beautiful person. I think at the time one rather wished that she wasn't an officer and I began to think of her as mine. In those days, you weren't, a mere Leading Seaman, allowed to fraternize with an Officer. Despite her rank, she spoke equally, as it were, to all of us, ratings and officers. Having welcomed each of us as we arrived over the day she disappeared into another part of the house.

She, my brown-eyed Wren officer, was there again along with other members of her team when we were briefed about the next mission. Even now I remember that briefing as clearly as if it were yesterday. The crew were all gathered together, we hadn't seen our passengers yet, waiting to be told of our destination. Where were we going? OH NO! It was the same trip as last time. Back to La Rochelle! This time however we were not going to drop south of La Rochelle to Royan. This was to be a sea drop but quite close in to La Rochelle. I can remember feeling my heart speed up. Suddenly, I was beginning to have real fear, almost for the first time since I had been with this group. I had known fear before. In the cupboard under the stairs at home during the Battle of Britain and the bombings. During the dive-bombing attacks on the convoy run to Russian and back. But this time, as they said La Rochelle I felt afraid. Thinking about it now, perhaps it was a moment of panic. Maybe it was the beginning of a little bit of battle fatigue.

As the fear swept over me, I recall an equally powerful emotion. The sudden realisation that I was now seen as a veteran. This made it even more important to keep fear or any other emotion to myself, hidden and contained deep within. It wasn't just about the British stoicism. It was the recognition that uncontrolled fear and even other emotions can interfere with good decision making, particularly in those times of extreme demand and danger. A little fear is good thing as it heightens the senses, helping you be alert and on top of your game. But fear that becomes or moves towards panic is a very dangerous thing and I had just felt a twinge of panic!

In these more modern of times, with our greater insights of psychology and the functions of the brain, you can teach solders the skills necessary to master our natural fight or flight response. Or as it is sometimes called the 'freeze response', which is in many ways is a better description for a military context. But in my time, the control came from ingrained beliefs and attitudes of what it meant to be a solider. Good old fashion military discipline.

The emotional recovery from my war, the Second World War, was I think, if in fact it's fair to describe it as such, easier than for those who were to fight in later conflicts such as Vietnam. We were fighting to defend our homes. We were fighting to defend our families and loved one. The whole community, almost to a person, supported, valued and even demanded that its young men and women fought. Even to this day most believe it was a just war. Yes, it's true that we were involved in many things which were unjust, and had we not been on the winning side, possible atrocities and even war crimes. But those who are the victors can choose to forget - yet let's hope we will never repeat some of the things that we did in the name of War.

We used to have some down time before we went on an operation. After my twinge of panic and in that interval, I decided to confide in my brown-eyed Wren office. I told her that I was really feeling a bit scared, a little unnerved about this trip. I wonder if I would have shared my apprehension with a male officer.

She said, "Do you know what they say about you in your records? You're the coolest character they've got. Thank goodness you have a small amount of human feeling." She continued, "You don't drink, you go to church, you don't go out with girls and you take whatever the Navy throws at you without saying a word."

Looking back on it, what she said to me at that time was perfect for the moment. It was okay to have some apprehension and fear of a mission; I was just normal. My brown-eyed Wren officer even hinted that because of these attributes, after my next trip, it would be noted in my official papers and I would be accredited as 'Mentioned in Despatches'. I remember my confidence being restored and likely, that's why she said what she did. The 'Mentioned in Despatches' never did eventuate; she was however a good coach.

The trip across, and then through, the Bay of Biscay was very like the former trip. The weather was a lot worse however, if that were possible, and delayed our progress more than anticipated. All these years later, I am not quite able to separate one trip from the other but I do remember thinking that it was a complete miracle that we weren't seen. When we finally spotted landfall we were much closer to La Rochelle than our first trip. The mission proceeded as planned and on this occasion, we did not unload our passengers in the harbour, but let them off while at sea, although close to shore. What makes this mission stand out is that we were carrying the first rubber-type dinghies that I had seen. I think that they would have been very much harder than the present ones, and much less flexible.

After the delay caused by the bad weather and the time it took for our operatives to be loaded, they disembarked and headed off to the shore just as it was nearing dawn. The first signs of light had not yet appeared. We knew from quite early in the mission that with the delays we would have to make a daylight run out of the Bay of Biscay. The mission would have been cancelled if the drop-off risked daylight but with all the calculations indicating a dark arrival and drop, a daylight run for home, although high risk, was just war. Having said that however, ships like ours, available for special missions, were difficult to find. I am sure our bosses, whoever they were, would not have wanted to lose the vessel either sunk or impounded. Sailors, I fear, were more expendable.

With the dinghies safely away, we waited in case an emergency pick up was required. After what seemed an eternity, we turned around and began heading out of the Bay. It was still darkness but the first signs of dawn were beginning to emerge on the horizon. The rather frightening daylight dash was about to start but to avoid any unnecessary attention, we lumbered along slowly, heading back out to sea. A Spanish merchantman leaving harbour at first light. We had not been sailing long when all of a sudden, the night sky lit up. Flares were being dropped on the horizon all the way around us followed by one close to our position. We couldn't see where the flares were coming from and like our last mission, most of our armaments had been removed. We had little chance of defending ourselves, let alone putting up a fight. Wearing civilian clothes, if caught we would be shot as spies. We were being hunted but luckily the sun had not yet broken the night sky and what remained of the dark was still our friend. The only defence we had at our disposal was to alter course, which we did, and to make sure our light armaments were well hidden but within easy reach. We could not afford to be intercepted as in all likelihood we would be shot. In keeping with our disguise, we pulled the collars of our dark coats up around our necks, wore our caps low upon our head and lumbered slowly on, not increasing speed despite the flares.

Luckily no other flares were to come anywhere near us and if they were looking for us, they didn't know where we were. Maybe they thought we were a submarine chaser, or maybe it was a German submarine leaving La Rochelle. We stayed on our new course and slipped slowly and quietly back out to sea as the first signs of dawn lightened the skies behind us.

With no other incidents, our return trip was apparently undetected, although we did hear the drone of aircraft - that familiar hunting sound of the enemy aircraft engines. I never did learn whether this was the Daimler Benz engine or the Junkers engine, but the people who were bombed in so many parts of the world will never forget that boom–boom-boom, boom-boom-boom sound of the engines.

We returned to England with no difficulties except some minor engine problems which were always expected but always unwelcome. On this occasion, we did not return to Cliff but sailed into Newlyn Harbour, Penzance. At Penzance, we were told that our mission was successful and once again, each of our crew departed to whence they came. I was to take the long train journey via Bristol up to Warrington. By then I had become a dab hand at having my travel and draft warrant ready to travel all over the place. Being shore based and in Britain, unlike those serving overseas, I seemed to have regular leave. Although I didn't drink and went to church, I wasn't really the saint I sometimes claimed. To travel from Warrington to Cliff and all the other ports of operation, I had been given a whole handful of travel warrants, some of which I didn't use. I managed to keep a half dozen or so and with my acquired warrants I could take myself on many a journey, a free train trip whenever I was on leave. I think it's called stealing, but at the time and even now, I think it was fair, although not right.

Chapter Ten
French Resistance

My next trip took me to Scotland and a place called Anstruther. It's a small fishing village about 9 miles south-east of St Andrews and a very beautiful place. Anstruther has always been a town steeped in mystery and secrets, from its early smuggling days to it involvement with the military and intelligence services during the second and cold wars. Now a major tourist attraction and hidden beneath what appears to be a Scottish farmhouse, a 24,000 square feet secret bunker gives testament to the government's interest and involvement in the area. The bunker, it is alleged, was built in case of nuclear war and was capable of housing 300 personnel and would have served as a seat of government and war room. It was hidden from the town's folk for over 40 years - like many of the activities that happened here during World War Two.

Arriving at Anstruther I went to its little harbour and after showing my pass, which was mandatory to gaining entry, I gained entry to the port. There were several minesweepers in dock and, I remember at that time, not an enormous amount of other activity. There was one D Class motor torpedo boat tied up. I looked around but couldn't see our vessel; the one we had taken on the last couple of missions. I spoke to a few people, but nobody seemed to know anything about me and I was just regarded with a look of blank amazement, so I thought I'd go aboard the MTB. I remember seeing the head of a person in the usual place where the watchman hid to keep out of the weather. It was raining hard at the time and I shouted out that I wished to come aboard. A voice said, "Yes, Sir."

It must have been my voice, my private school accent, because when he saw a Leading Seaman, he was a bit surprised. I told him I was not certain whether I was to report on this ship or not. I couldn't give him any details because I didn't know any and even if I did they would have been secret. He said that I had better see the officer of the watch and left me to find my own way. On my way down to the ward room, I noticed that this D Class had what appeared to be fuel tanks all the way along the upper deck. Having seen this layout before I immediately thought," *Ah, this is our vessel - looks like another long journey*."

When I went down below, the young midshipman who was onboard said, "Oh, you are two days early if you are who I think you are, Sir". I thought, "*this is unusual. He called me 'Sir' as well*", not that I minded. Being called 'Sir' was about as close to being an officer as I would be. What made it unusual however, was I was in my Leading Seamen uniform! He said, "You're with the Special Operations group".

I said, "Yes, that's correct!"

He said, "I understand you are all officers."

I said, "Thank you for that compliment, but I happened to be an officer of the non-commissioned type. We are a Special Operations group however, but, you understand, I can't say anymore".

He said, "Our job was just to transport – to bring the MTB here. We were instructed not to talk about it or to ask any questions".

They found room for me down in the aft, in what was the motor mechanics department. There appeared to be no motor mechanic, just a couple of stokers. I was onboard for a day and a half, when suddenly, there was a bit of a noise and some familiar faces and voices. This mission would be with our old crew which is always a great relief. Secretly I wondered if my favourite Wren would be coming as I was becoming particularly fond, even smitten, by her. I looked up and there she was, my brown-eyed Wren, standing on the dockside. I rushed out, all the while trying to appear unhurried, uninterested and surprised to see her.

She seemed genuinely pleased to see me and shouted, "Hello, Laurie!" calling me by my Christian name. Just as she did, the midshipman went by and hearing the Wren call the Leading Seaman by his Christian name, as he passed, he turned and saluted.

He said, "Goodbye Sir," and obviously thought the Leading Seamen uniform was a disguise. Just part of the Special Operations stuff.

Many years later, when I was a minister, in good fun, I told one of my fellow clergymen, himself an ex-service man, the story of the Wren and being saluted. To my surprise, he called me a "bloody liar!" So even clergymen can swear! But it did mean that for many years I kept my own counsel about this part of my war. I think if you even slightly hinted about being involved in some kind of clandestine special operations, people looked at you with a high degree of suspicion, as if to suggest you were being less than honest with the truth.

Thinking about my time on these operations, even to this day, it would be difficult, if not impossible, to confirm the specific stories. I believe we were working with and transporting members of the Special Operations Executive (SOE) and sometimes commandos, but I am not sure. There are well-documented records of the Royal Navy Coastal Forces' work with the SOE, transporting agents to France and Belgium. It is well known however that Royal Navy groups working with the SOE, or other Special Operations, often worked in isolation of each other. For security reasons, one would conclude. Although I haven't undertaken any detailed research since the war, from time to time after the war, I did look out for stories of our particular missions, if only to help me remember. The answers were to be found but not where you might think.

Well, this was to be another aborted run. We took the D Class MTB out on trials and went up the coast towards Dundee. Again, we had engine trouble and the motor mechanic said to the First Lieutenant, "This is ridiculous, they've done it on us again."

He said, "They've sent us their rubbish because they know we are likely to lose it." Whatever the job was, it was cancelled before even our guest had arrived. It still, however, appeared to count as trip number six.

Number seven was to be the most secretive and daunting of all our trips. Over four days, we would sail our vessel to Belgium, dock it in an enemy port, I would kill two people with my bare hands, all to safely deliver our passengers on a mission to find and eliminate (kill) a French Resistance leader, one of our allies, all under the guise of the Germans.

We were sent down to the south. The port of embarkation was the little town of Wivenhoe, just south of Colchester in Essex on the river Colne, which runs down to Brightlingsea and out into the North Sea. The ship again was a long-range version of a D Class MTB. Unlike some of our previous operations there was no time given to fully familiarise ourselves with the new vessel before we set sail. Like one of our previous trips, a new petty officer coxswain who had not travelled with us before was appointed to our team with the duties of steering the ship. But unlike the former time when a coxswain was appointed, this petty officer asked no questions. Now a veteran of six missions, I was not concerned this time that I had lost my role in the team.

Despite the secrecy surrounding this operation and unlike some of our previous trips, we could go ashore (into town) prior to leaving on the mission. However, it is fair to say, we had not yet been briefed, so when we went into town, we did not know where we were to be sent. But as we were now an experienced team, I'm sure the hierarchy was confident in our silence.

The call-up for this trip (number seven) was a little unusual for when it came; they asked that we bring our civilian clothing. The Navy supplied us with civilian clothing for these trips and I remember when I first joined the team how surprised I was to be given a lot of civvy clothes including a pair of nice grey trousers that I kept. We were also given on most trips white Naval polo-neck jerseys, of which I accumulated a large number and even after the war, I still had several of them. As most of our trips had been made in civilian clothing, it was unusual to be asked specifically to bring them which is why I remember this call up. My mother, the reserved and quiet super sleuth, was surprised, if not suspicious, that the Navy was providing me with civilian clothes. And even more surprised by the number of jerseys I started to accumulate. Packing for Wivenhoe, I remember my mother looking on warily at my civilian clothing. I said something like, "Sometimes I get a chance to change in the toilets when I get a spot of shore leave from the training depot". Although, with all confidence I can say she did not accept my explanation, the type of activities we were engaged in would never have entered her mind.

So, those of us who were now considered veterans of a few operations, even though nothing had happened on the majority of them, were allowed to go ashore in Wivenhoe. I remember thinking, *"What am I going to do?"* I thought I would go to the pictures. In my civilian clothes, whom should I meet up with, also in civvy clothes and looking most beautiful, but my brown-eyed Wren Naval officer? She simply said when she saw me, "What are you going to do?"

We didn't go to the movies, but just walked together, talking. We talked not about the missions, but the war and our dreams for a future after the war. The military uniform locks away the vulnerabilities and aspirations of its wearer. You are the person of the uniform, the gentleness of the secret inner soul, hidden and protected from the realities and brutality of war. And so, in our civilian clothes, we walked and talked and, if only for a moment in time, we were two ordinary people again. After what seemed a long but enjoyable time, we finished up at a nice hotel having a quiet and I would like to recall, intimate, meal together. Of course, in those days, it was absolutely forbidden for a rating to take an officer out but no one was to know.

Even though I was very much naïve when it came to the ways of women, when she held my hand and looked into my eyes and said, "We are not due back until the morning", I knew the door was wide open for me to spend the night with my brown-eyed Wren; a woman who had made my heart skip since the very first time I saw her. I could be dead by the end of the week and she was stunningly beautiful; that smile and that auburn flowing hair. Was it because I had never been with a woman before? Maybe it was because she was an officer and I a rating. Or was it that my belief didn't support sex out of marriage?

I don't know, but after a long pause, I said, "I had better make my way back to the ship."

She refused to let me pay and handed the money over to me, saying, "On your pay, it's very difficult." I suppose it was.

Later in life I was to become an ordained minister of the Anglican Church and married my beautiful wife. Looking back, I am now glad that I didn't submit to temptation that night; although I suppose that makes me uninteresting, doesn't it? But where does virtue hide when mortality beckons and the veil of what is right and just becomes a cryptic illusion? It was okay to kill someone with my bare hands, but sex? That was out. By modern standards, it was, perhaps, strange, but I am always glad that I didn't sleep with my brown-eyed Wren that night, and particularly after a twist that was to happen about a year later.

When I finished my tour with the Special Operations group and with it, my duties as an instructor, I was sent down to the Motor Torpedo Depot, and who should be there? My brown-eyed Wren, who was looking more beautiful than ever. We greeted each other like old friends as she was just getting off one of the trot boats, as they called them. They used the trot boats to visit the other boats in Portsmouth Harbour and to take you to HMS *Vernon,* which was a depot on the far side of the water at Portsmouth, because the Motor Torpedo Depot was at Hasler. I noticed that she was wearing an engagement ring on her finger, which I commented upon. She said yes, she was getting married. Watching us talking was a Lieutenant Commander. He oversaw the drafting department. It was strange, but within twenty-four hours, I was drafted for a short stint minesweeping, but then to vessels which in many ways, carried on the pattern of going behind the enemy lines that I got used to in Special Operations. I don't, in hindsight, think I was sent to ships doing special operations because the Lieutenant Commander wanted me well away when he saw the sparkle in his fiancée's brown eyes when we met, but at the time, I was sure that was the case. It's amazing the conspiracies we can create in our own mind and then find all the evidence we need to prove them. Perhaps the answer lies in the power of a man's jealousy. The conspiracy was, of course, total rubbish; duties were just duties. After the war, the Lieutenant Commander and I shared a good friendship, which was to last fifty years. But what of my brown-eyed Wren who was by then his wife? Perhaps that's a story for another time but not a very interesting one. We all move on but I think most of us have memories of an old sweetheart, a memory quite dear because it was never quite true which permits us to, at times, play with a fantasy which can never be challenged by the realities of life.

The operation from Wivenhoe was to take us across the minefields in the North Sea to the Belgian coastline in an area not too far from Ostend. Our mission was to land a group of operatives that we carried onboard. Unlike previous occasions, I had not instructed any of this group so the harbour was my first encounter with them. Like those who had gone before them, they kept very much to themselves and other than the courtesy of a nod of acknowledgement, no other engagement was to be had. On some drops, our passengers had been relatively lightly armed, on this occasion however they were well equipped but not as some might have expected. This mission was not to be without its challenges. This was not to be a sea drop, so we had to get inside a harbour as these operatives and their equipment were to be dropped on land, and then being the kind of people they were, they would simply disappear into the night to carry out their mission.

It's a relatively short trip across the channel from Wivenhoe to Belgium and I remember the conditions were perfect - perfect for sailing but not for cover. I don't know, or I can't now remember, the name of the actual place where we made port. It was however, a very small harbour somewhere on the Belgium coast. In the dark of night, we simply sailed our vessel slowly and purposely into port and tied up. One can only assume that our intelligence sources had suggested that this was likely an unguarded small fishing harbour - of no strategic significance. Regardless, the tension on the boat was palpable.

As I climbed from the boat up onto the wharf, to my absolute horror, I was standing an inch or two away from a German armed guard. We were, of course, like all our missions, not dressed in Navy uniform. I can still see him with a rifle on his shoulder as he looked at me and I gave a cursory nod of my head and just walked by. He clearly was not expecting any trouble, let alone, a Royal Navy vessel to be in the harbour. Then I saw another guard approaching. Our operatives were now beginning to disembark and walk off into the dark. There was too much movement, and too many people for such a small port. Surely the guards would notice. They would know or sense something was not right. I paused, unsure of what was to happen and what I was to do. I knew the first guard was now just feet behind me, with another guard approaching. *"Was I to go back? Was I to get back on the motor torpedo boat?"* I continued to move slowly forward and I heard a German voice. The approaching guard said something, and I smiled. He was inquisitive, not alarmed, as he made no attempt to unshoulder his gun. Then I heard this guttural-toned voice from the MTB Bridge that said, "Kill him!"

I was now only a matter of feet from the second guard. Projecting my body forward, I delivered a sharp and powerful punch to his throat, my momentum bringing me alongside this young German soldier. I placed my hands around his head and, using the leverage from our combined body weights, I gave a sharp twist and his neck snapped. His body went limp. The young guard did not defend himself and it was all over too quickly for him to do so. I had killed the first person I ever knowingly killed with nothing but my own hands. As I broke his neck, the body fell over the wharf, missing our ship and dropping into the water. The splash was deafening in the silence of the night.

Remembering the first German guard, I turned quickly. I could just see him; he became clearer as he moved towards me, but he was still unsure what was happening. He stopped, perhaps ten feet away, looking at me almost as though he were saying, "Vot is dis?" You know, "Who are you? What is going on?" He was probably looking for the other guard and confused by the sound of something falling into the water. He began moving his rifle from his shoulder. The distance between us was too great; I couldn't disarm and kill him before he had time to raise the alarm and get off a shot. The success of our mission was dependent upon silence, no alarms and no gunshots. Our operatives needed time to vanish undetected into the night. Two other members of our crew had, by this time, come up onto the wharf behind the guard. One of them gave him a rugby tackle and he fell where I was. I remember putting my hand over the steel helmet and pulling back sharply, as we had been taught, and hearing his neck break. He was dead, limp. I let his head fall to the ground where his body was lying from the tackle. We left him on the wharf. We didn't throw him in the water because of the noise, and in the dark, we weren't sure where our boat was below.

Our operatives had finished disembarking by this time and were moving quickly, but stealthfully off into the dark of night. We climbed back onto our boat, started the motors and began moving off. Being a small harbour, in the darkness, it took what seemed a lifetime to reverse and turn around. It would not take long for the guards to be missed, and the dead body on the wharf to be found. Our time for escape was going to be limited. First, single machine guns, then more machine guns fired on us from all sides of the harbour. Unlike some of our previous missions when our guns had been removed so we looked like a merchantman, this time, we were in an armed MTB. We closed up our guns, but did not fire back. The fire from shore was very erratic and the order from our commander was given to hold our fire. It was a dark night and the Germans couldn't see clearly where we were. A couple of flare canisters were thrown in the water, which lit up a small area of the harbour and seemed to attract most of the machine gunfire as we quietly slipped out and disappeared into the night. As we motored away, you could still see tracer going into the area where we had been. It's funny what stays with you. I still remember the green tracer; I had never seen a green tracer, which the Germans were using.

After escaping the harbour all that was in front of us was to safely return home. It was about halfway across the North Sea when we closed up to action stations. Although I had not, on this trip, done an enormous amount of the steering, the CO asked for me to take the helm while we were in action stations. Meanwhile, he and the petty officer manned two of the twin Vickers machine guns from the side of the bridge. An E-boat appeared out of the darkness and, with our boats training their guns on each other, slipped slowly by, without firing a single shot. Later, when I was to serve on MTBs in the Coastal Forces, we could go out for nights searching for the enemy without coming across a single E-boat. In Coastal Forces, you were to 'seek and destroy'. Our missions however, were to 'sneak and avoid'.

As we slipped by, we knew it would be highly unusual for there to be only one E-boat and it did not take long to realise that we were among quite a few as they came and went in the dark. You can only imagine the tension on board our boat. Completely outgunned, we were not going to be the ones to initiate a firefight. Suddenly, the flash of a signal lamp broke the darkness. Somebody flashed at us, followed almost immediately by a burst of very accurate bullets, which hit the ship down the side. It was obvious to all of us that we were being fired on by another D Class MTB and the E-boats we were among were not firing, probably because they were trying to slip quietly away from the patrolling Coastal Forces. We were now at huge risk of engaging with what we thought was our own side.

I don't recall exactly how it happened, perhaps with a great deal of luck, we put on our navigation lights and fortunately, we were right. It was our own side shooting at us. With an element of luck, we safely transferred from being the foe to our side without too much more difficulty, and returned to tell the story. Being tenuously hidden amongst E-boats, which were being hunted by Coastal Forces and the risk of being shot and returning fire to both friend and foe, was a tricky experience. Although it was all over very quickly, the memory of the event remained. Perhaps the mind has been kind to me. Although I never forgot killing the two Germans, that memory sat hidden buried below the E-Boats and other events of the war. It was many years later, when one night, at an event in Melbourne, as red and green laser lights darted like tracer bullets across the night sky, my thoughts were transported back to that Belgian harbour and the two young men I killed. As the memories bubbled to the surface, I pondered and prayed quietly for them and their families, and for that time, long ago, which seems to come closer as I age.

When we returned to our English base, and before we dispersed, I was to meet and spend some time once more with my brown-eyed Wren. I think because we had not slept together that night before our mission, the trust and intimacy between us had grown. For the first time, we talked openly of the mission and she was to share what had always been secret before and I was to learn why we were sent.

Our operatives were free French with a mission to attack a camp and assassinate a French Marquis Resistance cell leader. From what I can recall, apparently, there was trouble with a communist element of the Resistance, and the partisan movement in general. This was making it more difficult to unite the varying resistance factions. It was thought that this Marquis cell or a person within it had given information to the Germans which caused a significant setback for the allies a year earlier. It was thought that this cell could not be trusted considering the upcoming events. Time wise we were in the lead up to D-Day although I did not know this at the time and nor did she mention it.

We often now talk of the French Resistance as united and coordinated fighting cells. Nothing could be further from the truth. They were mostly independent groups with varying political beliefs and ideologies, some guerrilla groups and some nonviolent and they varied considerably in sizes. For whatever reason, the government now wanted this cell eliminated or, at least, some people in particular. My Wren told me that blowing up and destroying the camp was a subterfuge to muddy the true purpose of the attack. So, everything our operatives carried, the explosives, and of course, the weapons, were German. Our own operational instructions were to resist engaging or exchanging fire with the enemy at all costs. The operation was to give the appearance of the Germans attacking the Resistance. Again, rather like our Irish operation. It wouldn't have been the British that would have raided free France, would it? But unlike Ireland, this operation was at the request of the French who had provided the detailed intelligence necessary to carry out the mission. As to the success of the mission, and of the politics, I would never know.

Returning once again to instructor's duties, it was now the lead up period to D-Day. I think everybody was aware that something big was on the horizon as the training programme at the camp began to change dramatically. Training was now much more centred on weaponry and forming the trainees into a defence group should the Germans attempt to attack us in their effort to prevent the allies invading Europe. Even as an instructor, I had, at times, to sit through being taught how to strip down a machine gun, do basic military type movements and basic close combat. The change in training routine did, however, provide some welcome variety, as we spent time away from the camp on military exercises involving things like night operations, capturing the pretend enemies' soldiers and attacking their camp. We even got to work with the Home Guard at one place. However, I was not back at camp long when once again, I was released to go and see my old friend, Cliff.

The house at Cliff had become a very friendly place, having done most of the trips with the same crew. We met as old friends and, in fact, we were veterans and very proud of some of the things that we participated in. By now, our guardedness with each other had lapsed and we did occasionally talk of our missions. A strong bond had developed between all of us. Our new assignment was to drop our passengers off in the Netherlands. At the briefing, a barely visible, but noticeable to those within our team, sense of relief swept across the room when we learned that this was a sea drop, not another harbour landing. These people again were counter agents, or people who lived in that part of the world. We were to be sent somewhere near the Scheldt area, which I would get to know very well a little later in the war.

The pattern of our operations was now similar. We would go through the minefields, drop our people, this time, quite a few miles off the coast, then hang around for a while before heading home. Operation number eight was memorable for hiding in a minefield and watching a whole German coastal convoy go by.

The CO was just itching to get on the radio and say where they were, but we were on a secret mission landing people and nothing could be said. We reached the drop-off point and disembarked our passengers, all unchallenged. On the way back, we saw what we thought was a trawler but, as we caught up to it, it turned out to be an enemy vessel, which let off a few rounds in our direction but did not seriously challenge us. We did, as always, not want to engage and so did not return fire, simply altering our course and increasing speed. They ceased fire and did not pursue. We had another pretty uneventful return trip to England.

Trip number nine was a trip I will never forget for its madness. It was to be a one-way trip and a fight to the death. It was basically a suicide mission and that seemed to be its intent. Our team assembled once again, not at Cliff, but this time, at a house occupied by the Royal Navy near Broadstairs, not far from Margate Kent. At the briefing, we were assigned our duties, but unlike previous missions, we were told this was to be a very dangerous mission and that those who went had to be volunteers. Of course, everybody said yes, and the briefing continued with the briefing officer saying, "I take it you're all volunteers," which seemed a stupid statement. It reminds me now of the terms and conditions you must tick when downloading or installing a program on your computer. It's not consent for there is no real choice.

The operation was to be a raid on Calais, of all places. It was now early June 1944 and our task force of about three ships was to sail across the Channel undetected, then enter and attack Calais Harbour. We weren't at the time to know, but this was only a few days before 'Operation Overlord', the invasion of Europe. It appeared, with the benefit of hindsight, that our mission was to be a diversionary attack. The raid would make it appear that Calais was to be the principal landing place for the allies, or that the invasion had begun.

In the lead-up to D-Day, the allies had, on several occasions, sent a large number of ships, and some barges, close to Calais and then returned home. Like the raid on St. Nazaire, our ships were to carry commandos and other special services people. During the briefing, I was, for the first time, to hear our operations group called a Special Boat Section–SBS. The Royal Navy during the Second World War did have many Special Operation units and, whether we were part of the SBS only for this mission or if it was the name they chose to describe our task group for all of its missions, I will never know.

On this mission, we were to go into Calais with covering fire from several warships. The number of ships has faded with time, but the memory of "That's all?" still holds strong. One of the ships was a steam gunboat and the commander was the famous natural history author and painter, Peter Scott, who at the time was a lieutenant commander. He had a reputation for being bit of a tartar and a disciplinarian; fortunately, we were never to meet.

The orders were that our task group was to go in, disembark our commandos, engage the enemy with all ferocity, take on whatever attacked us and stay there as long as was possible. We were in effect to fight to the last man; there would be little chance of surrender and escape would be difficult, if not impossible as our ships would most certainly have been damaged. The enemy forces at a major harbour like Calais would always be strong but this was the lead-up to the invasion of Europe. Germany was reinforcing all its lines and they were ready to repel any invasion. This was, likely, to be a one-way journey.

After the briefing, what was, by now, quite a large contingent of men were gathered in a house. We weren't allowed to leave. All our usual backup people were there, even a company of Wren, including my brown-eyed friend. The departure and the attack were delayed because of the shocking weather, high winds and rain, but there was a clear forecast for the next day. So, we had what, at the time we believed, was to be our last night.

During war, you push death from your thoughts and welling mind by covering it with a thin veneer of "It won't happen to me," "I will survive," and "Victory will be ours." But here, the veneer had been scraped away, preparing for a battle where there was to be no victory, no surrender, but most likely a fight to the last man. We were due to go the very next day. The calm, the inner power, which had bottled our fear, love and grief, blew away like the violence of the wind that battered the house that night.

The girls who had, for over two years, been working with various Special Operations groups, sending men on dangerous missions, often not expecting them to return, once again prepared their men. But this time, they prepared them for certain death.

As night fell, the enshrouding darkness was filled by a raging wind and rain that beat upon our house like some primeval drum. It stirred and aroused, in men and women alike, the most basic and primitive of all human instincts. Men, some married, some not; women, some married and some not, surrendered to basic instinct in what was an explosion of passion, lust and sex.

I was not to have a woman that night, for I was not that kind of person. So, on what was to be perhaps my final night on earth, I had no partner and was alone. I was not trying to set a moral standard or be prudish; it was just the way I was. This group of people mostly knew each other and had worked closely together under exceptional circumstances and pressure. I was to gain, that night, an understanding of how people could give in to this closeness. Later in life, when I became a Marriage Guidance Counsellor in Australia, that night taught me about temptation and how it can stalk even the most unwilling of players. I learned that you need to control your circumstances and environment as much as the temptation itself. Don't place yourself in harm's way. Do this by keeping away from those situations where temptation can call to test your will and resolve.

The next morning, the mission was cancelled and the people, the men and women, had to return from that most primitive of places, coming back to normal or whatever normal was in a time of war. When the call to stand down and disband came, the sense of relief was fogged by a mixture of euphoria, embarrassment and guilt. But that night, when we all truly believed we were to be sacrificed for king and country, the normal rules, morals and values did not seem to apply.

Chapter Eleven
All Hands Lost

The next trip was to be another number nine, as the aborted Calais raid was not in the reckoning. It was to take place again in Belgium and the mission followed a similar pattern. We landed in Belgium and off-loaded our people all without incident, but for a small skirmish leaving the coast. Although we had been in hostile territory, sailed across the minefields and entered an enemy port, the trip was, for the best part, uneventful.

The final trip, number ten, was to take place in what seemed like months later and well after the D-Day landings. The destination was Ostend, Belgium, when the summer of 1944 was fading and autumn was soon to be on the rise. With the allied troops on land slowly moving up the coast, our job was to deliver operatives into the still occupied harbour city of Ostend and, while there, pick up some 'special people'. It seems unbelievable that we could sail into Ostend itself unchallenged. Tying up at the dockside we could see a rather modern, round-shaped glass building, which, a few months later, would house many MTBs. In hindsight, it must have been very close to the liberation of Belgium which may help explain the lack of interest in our presence, but we, or least I, did not to know that at the time.

To enter Ostend, we had to sail past the battery located north of the harbour. The battery was equipped with four 105-millimetre guns. The fortress at Ostend was built during World War One and rebuilt as part of the German Atlantic Wall that ran along the Western Coast in anticipation of an allied invasion from Britain. The entrance to the harbour was quite narrow, so our strategy, like the missions before, was to bob along like nothing was out of place. For any observer, we belonged and obviously posed no threat. We landed in Ostend and even went for a walk around the area while dropping off our agents and picking up some other people. Our job was to get these people as fast as possible back to England. On returning to England, we didn't stop at the coast; we went right the way up the Thames to the Westminster Pier, to the heart of London. It was there that our guests departed, to be greeted by some very stern and official looking people. In keeping with the secrecy of all our missions, no words were spoken or ideas exchanged either during or after the voyage. Were they going straight to Parliament? I don't know and I will never know, but you would think that might be the most likely explanation.

Perhaps, by my final trip, overconfidence was beginning to take hold. Not only were we prepared to sail into an occupied harbour, but even take time for a stroll. Was it arrogance? Or just the boldness you need to complete missions with a statistically higher chance of failure than success? Neither may be the whole truth. Perhaps a casual stroll is the memory's way of dealing with the pressure, tension and reality of the actual events. For much of what happened in war, I remember a confident and self-assured me; but of more recent times, I find my past more tainted and less certain.

I returned to the naval base, the training camp outside Warrington, to be told that my time as an instructor had come to an end and, with it, my time in Special Operations. I had completed ten operations with Special Services, or whatever we were called and was now about to start the next phase of my war. A strong and powerful bond had developed between the members of our team. I experienced both a sense of relief and loss at the news my time had come to an end. We were all sworn to the strictest secrecy, so outside of the team, I couldn't share or reflect upon the experiences. After the war, many people harboured secrets, secrets of state, or perhaps personal secrets which hide what they or others did or saw. But most were the secrets of kindness, protecting those we loved, and perhaps ourselves, from the horrors of war and the scars we all carried.

I was soon to journey back to Portsmouth and, in an office in the Portsmouth barracks, I was confronted by the same Commander who started me on my journey.

He had once asked me, "What is it you would like to do? I believe you're qualified in all three spheres; would you like to do all three?" In calendar months, only a year had passed, but so much had happened. I was no longer the young, naïve person I was at the beginning: now an accomplished coxswain, a killer who could extinguish life using nothing but his hands. A keen observer of a secret part of the war often hidden from the eyes of others. There were several of us with the Commander, all instructors, but I believe I was the only one who had been on additional duties.

The Commander said to us, "I am sorry, but as you have been on instructional duties and have no seagoing experience, you must lose the rank of Leading Seaman which was given in recognition of your instructor's duties."

I remember almost bursting, "No seagoing experience!" The despair on my face must have betrayed my anger. The Commander looked at me, his eyes demanding but reassuring. I had to obey and I kept quiet as the others were leaving.

He said, "Oh, by the way, Biggs, may I have a word with you?" He continued, "I have to take away your rank, but the Leading Seaman will be off your papers for only one day and will be reinstated upon assignment to Coastal Forces." With an inflection of recognition in his voice he said, "I believe you have seen quite a bit of sea time," and gave an acknowledging nod.

My official papers, Certificate of Service, true to his word, show that I lost my Leading Seaman rank for indeed just one day but the papers are quite confusing. The best description I can muster is that they are altogether messed up. I was reinstated as a Leading Seaman the very next day when I was transferred, on paper at least, to HMS *Wildfire* in September 1944, albeit in an acting capacity. With the rank reinstated and like a regular rating in the Navy, I eventually took the Leading Seaman course that should have confirmed my rank, but my papers still had me down as 'Temporary Acting'. But it didn't matter that much and I was to continue with that rank until discharge in September 1946.

With my time as an instructor over, I was sent first to HMS *Hornet* at Gosport, headquarters for Coastal Forces to await draft to a vessel. It was there, as I have already related, that I met my brown-eyed Wren and, after talking to her too long on the dockside for the Lieutenant-Commander's pleasure, I was sent to a Coastal Forces flotilla of motor torpedo boats in Queenborough, near Sittingbourne in Kent. This was a unit trained for fast minesweeping. My reception upon arrival at the new boat was mixed. We were now in the latter part of the war and here I was, arriving, as it were, with only two Arctic convoys under my belt and then what appeared to the crew, a safe and comfortable life as an instructor. As an instructor, the crew thought I had been safe from the dangers of combat and those cold bleak nights on patrol, asleep each evening in my warm, comfortable and safe bed. This time, there was no one to say, "This man's been to Russia." To them, I was a novice. Perhaps lucky, but definitely green.

Our local multicultural TV station, SBS, recently ran a series of adverts about migrants and refugees coming to Australia. I remember in one, you saw an Indian man driving a taxi and the voice-over saying, "In his home country, this man is a doctor, lawyer, or was it an architect?" The profession matters not; but it was for me a powerful image. We see only the taxi driver and not the truth of and in this person. We don't know him, but still we are happy to make our subjective assessments and cast judgement none-the-less. That narrative in many ways was my story when I left the Special Services. That first day arriving at my new vessel was to have a profound influence in the coming years. After the war, I made it my endeavour to see and seek out the unique and special story of those I knew and met. Did I succeed? Perhaps not, for our eyes tend to see the world as we often wish or expect to see it and our egos have a habit of distorting our perceptions even further. But at times, I was rewarded and saw beyond the taxi driver to the untold story and was forever richer for doing so.

Thinking about my draft at the end of my Special Operations, I am reminded of my D-Day story. Laurence Biggs, the conquering hero - 'Captain Pug Wash, and his rowboat'.

For D-Day I was sent to Newhaven where I met a signalman, an able seaman, and a leading stoker. Together we were given a converted Harbour Defence Motor Launch and told, along with several people who also had cutters that we were to go out into the channel and await further instructions. During the D-Day landings, while men and machines battled the shadow of death for a foothold in Europe, we simply sailed out into the channel and bobbed around on what was a pleasant sixth day of June 1944. Our role, which we did not know at the time, was small, but none-the-less important. We were, as it were, the Dunkirk Boys. If anything had gone terribly wrong with the landings, we were on standby to go over and start the evacuation of troops.

Of D-Day itself, I saw nothing, and heard nothing except one American Liberator bomber, flying low in the sky, which appeared to be in trouble. One of my colleagues, I think it was the stoker, said he thought it was running on three engines and not four. The plane let a stick of bombs go; they probably landed in the sea, two or three miles away, but you could still feel the thud through the bottom of our boat as they hit the water and exploded.

At the end of what was quite a pleasant day, we returned to Newhaven and were greeted by all the shore people, waving and yelling as if we were conquering heroes. They thought we were the first people back from Normandy. Upon our return, we learned there had been a successful D-Day landing, and in my mind, all that occupied me was, *"Thank God the operation to Calais was called off!"* So as for D-Day, I could, in all honesty say, I was in command of one of the evacuation vessels. But the literal truth is not always the actual truth. So, I remain 'Captain Pug Wash and his rowboat,' prayerful for all the sacrifices of that day, and what was, for me, a pleasant day bobbing about in the channel.

The time spent at Queenborough was focused on learning about the different types of minesweeping gear and how to undertake comparatively high-speed minesweeping, a hazardous activity. We learned about single and double sweeps, Oropesa and Otters and what an Explosive Cutter was. The objective of minesweeping is to cut the mooring cable of the mine. This causes the mine to float to the surface, where it can be destroyed. The Otter pulls the cable and cutter towards and away for the ship. The Oropesa keeps the towed sweep at a determined depth and position from the sweeping ship. The sweep wire is kept down to the required depth by means of the kite, the wire being kept out from the ship by means of the Otter, attached to which is the Oropesa float. The original minesweeping equipment we had was, in the politest and the most British description I can give, unsuccessful or bloody useless for anybody else. As soon as we got up any speed, the system used to trip and we would have to stop.

Our job as minesweepers was to go ahead of the main fleet clearing and making safe the way. Eventually, we were lucky enough to get hold of some captured German minesweeping gear which was installed on-board our vessel. The superior German equipment allowed us to run at our maximum speed. It's difficult to argue that the Germans were not exceptional engineers. The theory with high speed minesweeping was, if you could run fast enough, you would not be struck by acoustic mines and, when they went off, you would be safe; well clear of them. Life on a minesweeper is a story in itself, but a quick one, for I was to have only a short stint at this time but would return to minesweeping at the end of the war. Mines, both at sea and on land, remain a significant hazard long after the war had finished.

While on this first posting, I was to be part of the minesweeping of Scheldt, where two hundred and seventy-six mines were cleared from the water, opening the river Scheldt to shipping, and giving access to the port of Antwerp. Although Antwerp had, by now, fallen to the British, the approaches to it along both banks of the Scheldt River were held by a heavily fortified German Army. The Germans did not want the allies gaining access to the port of Antwerp. The battle of Scheldt raged from September to November 1944. The minesweeping happened once the river was secured; however, we were still to lose one of our ships, ML *916*.

It was whilst I was at Queenborough that I bumped into one of the officers who was on the Special Services trips with me. When he saw me, he came over and said, "Did you hear the news?"

I said, "No, what news?"

He said, "Well, you and I are the only survivors from our team. They went on another operation. You and I had been taken off by then and all hands were lost. They all died." My heart sank and I can't explain the feeling as an emptiness filled the void where it once beat: *"all hands lost"*. Over the year, even though we only met to undertake missions, our group had developed a resolute bond. The fact that we all went our separate ways after each operation only seemed to strengthen the camaraderie. We were, in truth, I think deceived by our own invincibility. Although we were told that we were on highly dangerous and secretive missions, we went out and came back, nobody was injured, let alone killed and, for the most part, our trips had been uneventful.

I had seen death, I had seen war, but I was still totally unprepared for the news - not one or two, but *all gone*. It's hard to understand why some live and some die and you cannot help, but once again, be reminded of the role fate plays. Perhaps, as I was bobbing about in the channel on what was for me a pleasant enough day, they were behind enemy lines, sailing into an occupied port, a Spanish merchantman, a disguise once too often worn.

It was to be many years later, almost a lifetime, before I would see them all again. One night, in what was not quite a dream, they came to tell me that my time here on earth was drawing to an end and I would soon be joining them.

After the news of my colleague's deaths, as if in protest, I removed my metal identification tag or Dog Tags, as they became better known thanks to the Americans. The metal identification tags are worn by military personnel and used primarily to identify the deceased. I was not going to die and, from that moment forward, I wore my tags no more.

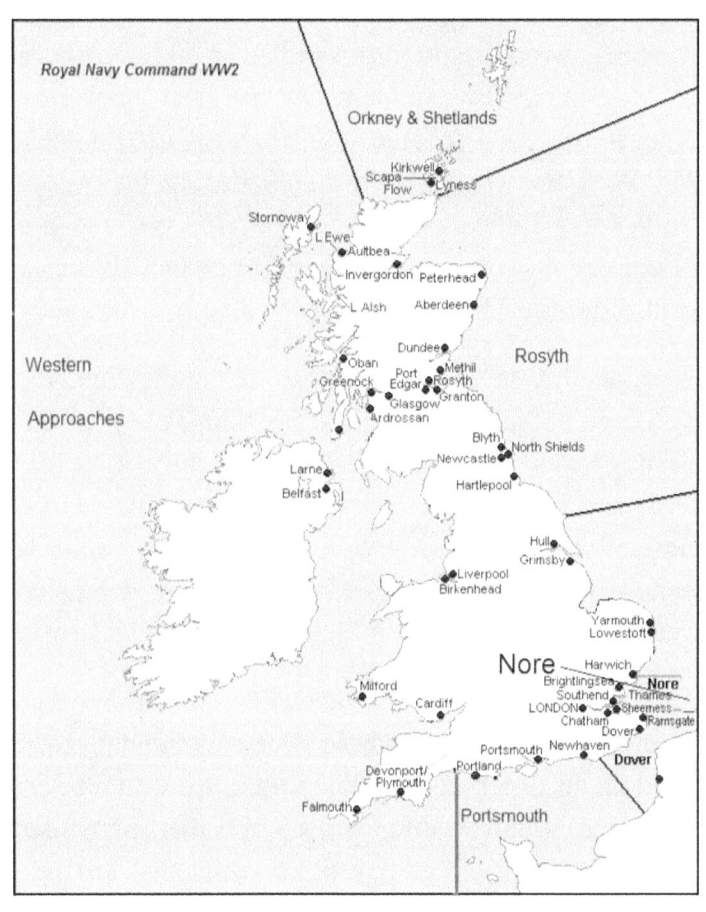

Being stationed on a high-speed Coastal Forces boat, besides minesweeping, we quite often got pulled in to escort convoys to France. After the D-Day landings, and the clearing of most of the French coast, we used to meet our convoys off Southend Pier. Southend Pier, known as HMS *Leigh* during the war and the surrounding area known as HMS *Westcliff*, was the mustering point of convoy movements for Nore Command. It was also the Navy control for the Thames Estuary.

Nore Command was responsible for defending the North Sea Coast and even had its own admiral, Sir John Tovey in 1944. The Royal Navy was apportioned geographically for its global commands and had six home defenced commands. Orkney and Shetlands, Rosyth, Nore, Dover, Portsmouth and Western Approaches. The Home Command controlled the defensive forces with vessels including motor torpedo boats, destroyers and minesweepers.

The CO used to go away to where ever commanding officers go and picked up his orders for the day. Often, we would be escorting merchant ships, usually sailing on the ebb tide, particularly if it was near evening. Even at this time, with much of the French coast in Allied control, we set sail near dusk thus allowing us to pass Calais in the dark of the night so that any of the guns still there would have difficulty firing on us. We did several trips around Calais, leaving our return convoys soon after Dungeness, all uneventfully. We never ran across any enemy ships as they were now operating further up the coast.

Occasionally, we were sent out on what was known as Z-line patrol–I love that name 'Z'. These patrols had nothing to do with any kind of Special Operations. We used to go into the minefields, particularly into the enemy minefields, to hide and observe any ship movements and report them back. Our role was not to attack but just stealthfully observe, report our findings and return to harbour. Other times, we just did repair and maintenance works on minesweeping equipment. Our patrols and duties then varied, depending on the day's orders. Much of the day to day activities of war are dull and boring, a routine which would be of no interest to a reader.

Returning from operations, we were often very tired as the trip up the Thames to reach Sheerness and Queenborough was a comparatively long one, particularly as the first part was at restricted speed. The restricted speed was in place because of an American ship. The SS *Richard Montgomery* was full of explosives (3,172 Tonnes) and had ran aground and then sunk off Sheerness. It was visible from the North Kent Coast and Southern Beach at low tide. All ships were speed-restricted so that the wakes and vibrations of the passing vessels did not disturb it and cause an explosion. It posed, at the time, a considerable threat to navigation. The Americans blamed the British for poor harbour control, which was indeed the conclusion of the inquiry. The Brits blamed the Americans for having nobody on watch as the ship dragged anchor and, despite the nearby ships sending warning of the impending danger, drifted onto the sand bank. The SS *Richard Montgomery* and its explosives still rest on the sand banks today.

It would be on one of these Coastal patrols that I was to have the first of those experiences which would set in place the foundations for my life after the war and the journey towards God.

The pace of war is a high mix of waiting and uneventful, almost boring routine, peppered with moments of ferocious intensity, only to settle once again into the mundane. On any given nightly patrol, you were more than likely to see nothing, but war is the uncertainty. Unfortunately, I was to remember this night well, when death called and fate would once again have its part to play.

Our mission that night would send us quite near the Dutch coast, which was almost our maximum range, there and back, without modified fuel tanks. I well remember it was a foul-weather evening. Winter was closing in and it was particularly cold, wet and miserable. I recall putting on the warm clothing, which we all had by this time, and I used to put a towel around my neck, a trick I learned on my Special Operations. It would stop the water from going down your neck. Quite often, there was greasepaint, which you could use to cover your face to try and protect you from the salt water spray. Once you got up to any speed in these ships, the spray flew wildly over the open bridge.

By now, a lot of my time was spent on the wheel even though I wasn't the coxswain. I was the second coxswain on this vessel. I had not long relieved the coxswain and was steering when the CO came to me and said, "I'm afraid if we run into trouble, you'll have to go and look after one of the guns. We have several sailors ill." It was not that long afterwards, while still at the wheel, when a message was received that enemy ships were in the area and we *closed-up* to action stations. I was relieved by the coxswain and took the Oerlikon 20-millimetre cannon amidships. My assistant was a Scottish chap called Jock. He was the loading number, not a trained gunner, but very strong. Of all the people on the ship, we did not get on. We *closed-up* and went on our Z patrol, lolloping and rolling all over the place, looking for enemy ships. With spray from the waves breaking over the ship and dousing us, we began to talk.

It was Sunday night. The two most terrifying and frightening nights in my life were to be Sunday nights. And this was one of them.

Jock said, "What would you be doing if you were at home?"

I said, "Sunday evening (forgetting that the blackout would not have allowed it) we would probably be going to church."

He laughed and said, "What good does that do?"

I said, "I like it. I like the music, the atmosphere, and it's nice to think that there are people out there perhaps singing for those in peril on the sea and offering up their prayers."

"What good would that do?" he said again. Then there was a silence. He turned to me and said, "Hooky, (referring to the anchor on my arm) I did a robbery and I think the cops are after me. I stuck a knife into somebody. I don't know if they died and I don't care. What does your church say about that?"

I don't recall what my exact answer was, but I do remember saying something like, "If you truly say you're sorry, we are taught - we believe that it can be forgiven." *Did I need to be forgiven for the people I killed? Or is war different?*

"The police may not forgive you, but above and beyond us all, there is this power that we believe in and it's this power in which we trust."

As I said this, the ship lurched, and it rolled forcibly. An ammunition box broke loose and pinned my leg to the side of the gun turret. It shouldn't have been there. It should have been in the ready use locker. I tried to remove it from my leg, but I couldn't and my leg was hurting badly. I shouted over the intercom to the bridge that the ammunition box had broken loose and my leg was pinned. I asked permission for Jock to take my place on the gun while I removed it.

"Permission granted" came the reply. I bent down and picked up the ammunition box and was placing it in the ready to use locker. Jock was now standing over me at the gun. I had a fearful sense that something went 'plonk!' and at the same time, I was soaking wet. It hadn't felt like the cold of the sea washing over me. This wet was warm.

Jock, standing where I should have been, had been shot in the head. It must have been the first-round out of probably a 20 millimetre, which had blown his head completely off. It was his blood which now poured down over me, warm and sticky.

Death, a constant companion who lurked in the shadows of war, never that far away, found Jock that night and not me. Did death, yet again, miss its mark in those few seconds when we had traded places? Was death cheated? Or had I been spared? Does God do that? Or was it just the random dice of fate, tossed and then falling in the seeming chaos of God's grand design?

Yet again, I had survived.

Gunfire and tracers penetrated the darkness, the exchange coming from all directions. I can't remember undoing the belt, which strapped Jock to the gun, but I must have done. His body fell away as I took up position to where, but a few seconds ago, I should have been. Suddenly, looming from the night and now at close range was an E-boat. I could see every shot as if the whole exchange was through my eyes.

'Concentrated accurate fire, I taught as an instructor, is the difference between life and death.' You don't unleash Oerlikons in one continuous stream. Instead you send out frequent bursts of focused fire. As I pulled that trigger, if ever I had reason to pray those sixty rounds would find their mark and go into that ship, it was now. The attack was soon over, as with many exchanges, it was intense, but short. We saw two other ships and again, quick and violent fire was exchanged before we each slipped away into the dark of the night.

The next thing I knew, I was being violently sick. With the exchange over, I was relieved, going down between the decks to wash. I was covered in blood which leached and soaked my whole being. I threw away all my clothes and changed into loan clothing. Remaining motionless, I was again overwhelmed by sickness and my thoughts. The passage of time for me came to a complete stand still. But only minutes really passed before once again, I had to return to action stations. Survival allows no room for grief or self-pity until the emptiness of the mundane patrol returns to be filled by a mind now free to roam.

Jock was dead. Yet, amazingly just before Jock died, I explained what forgiveness was. Was this part of my mission in life?

Jock had said, "Would they be praying for us now?"

And I said, "Yes."

He said, "You know, I believe……" and those were his last words. He believed what? Or was it 'I believe!' Was this another vision like St. Paul's sudden conversion? I shall never know, but I hope in quiet prayer that those sins Jock said he harboured were forgiven and he was at peace with his God.

Was it possible that perhaps once again, somebody was saying, "If I spare you from this war, I have a job for you to do and, one day, this will be one of the stories you will tell."

It's funny, as a priest, you cannot help but believe in the power of prayer. But how can you harbour a God who intervenes and who determines who will live and who shall die? If you did, how could you resolve all the good people, the holy and the righteous from of all faiths and religions, who die before their time, while those who some may describe as not so good, go on to live long lives?

In this time of the Second World War with the Holocaust in Europe, where so many, the Jews, Gypsies and the disabled perished, how can you reconcile a loving God who stands idly by? Perhaps he is watching in despair and weeps in sorrow? Does he choose and, if he does, how can this be? How can I resolve that I would pray for mercy, for my life to be spared, but for my bullets to find their mark? How could I believe that I had been spared because God had a job for me to do but, at the same time, know that a loving God, my God, would not choose?

Only one other person, the late Hugh Herbert, Vicar of St. Phillips Church, Norbury, South London and later of the church in Coulsdon, knew the story of Jock. The Archbishop ran an appeal at the end of the war to raise money to try and help people get back on their feet. To contribute to getting the economy going again, I donated a month's pay, along with a letter explaining the story. We were then to meet many times and developed a great understanding and became good friends. It was he who helped me make sense and find peace from the confusion of fate and faith. A confusion which is ever present, but more so during and in those early years after the war. I am not sure if it was Hugh Herbert who introduced me or I was to read the line much later from David O. McKay, a religious leader who said, "The greatest battles of life are fought out daily in the silent chambers of the soul." It's a pertinent line. After the war, when just facing the daily routine of civilian life seemed challenging, I learned that we must all seek inner peace. To reach an understanding of self and, in so doing, define your own unique mission in life.

German E-Boats

Chapter Twelve

Journey to God

It seems hard to believe that, after having served on the Russian convoy route and with Special Services, the real action was to be found here in ordinary units of Coastal Forces of the Royal Navy. We were involved in several surface actions and, considering there were only about four hundred and fifty service actions in the North Sea during the war, we were certainly having our fair share. They were however, on patrol duty, mostly minor skirmishes, not that we were becoming complacent as the end of the war neared and our anticipation of victory grew.

I have always, even before the war, had a keen interest in machinery; steam trains, boats and airplanes in particular. I liked the numbers, routines and timetabling and noting anything that was different or out of the ordinary. As you may recall, one of my duties on the convoys was aircraft recognition, so I remember the time when, on one of our daylight patrols, a very fast plane went whistling overhead. It was a plane that I did not recognise and was obviously something new from the German arsenal. I tried to remember and keep an image of the plane so I could, at a later time, attempt to identify it. It would take until after the war, but I have always wondered if it was a Me262, the German jet fighter. I could never be certain, but how exciting if I had seen one of these rare planes. What I do know is that it was being chased by a Tempest, with another plane diving out of the sky ahead of it, possibly an American P-51 Mustang. It was an amazing sight, but despite German advances in technology, the balance of the war had well and truly changed. Sir Frank Whittle of Britain is acknowledged as the co-inventor of the jet engine although the

Brits and Germans developed their technology independently of each other. Britain first flew a jet fighter in 1941 and, if the war had continued, the ability to counter the Me262 existed.

It's difficult, if not somewhat immoral, to seek the positives in conflict, but war does accelerate technology and the jet engine would revolutionize air travel and opened the skies to the masses. The German V2 rocket would eventually lead, in 1969, to man walking on the moon; a feat not repeated since Apollo 17 in 1972, the sixth landing. Unfortunately, it would also underpin the development of the ballistic missile, and with the Second World War also giving us the atomic bomb, we were to enter the new age with a new and deadly combination. Missiles armed with nuclear bombs. The new era was perhaps best summed up by the phrase, 'mutually assured destruction' (MAD). Most disturbingly, this became accepted military doctrine; 'how mad!'

In November, we took part in the mine sweeping of the Scheldt, and as I have said, lost another ship that was with us. The feeling of leading a sweep is indeed nerve-racking. You have several lookouts, waiting to see the signs of a mine, which is, no doubt, well below the water line and, if you are the ship in the lead, you are the one who is most likely to hit the moored mine. The other ships are strung out to one side or the other of yours. They normally seem to be to starboard, the right-hand side, each one being covered by the mine sweep of the ship in front. But if you are number one, as occasionally we were, it was absolutely nail biting. The normal leader was a motor launch, a fast one, number *250*, and the captain, who became a lieutenant commander, got the DSC for his troubles. Although, there weren't many medals dished out to people for these operations. This was just routine. If you released a mine and one came up - that entitled you to put a chevron on your ship.

Prior to the minesweeping of Scheldt, I was to take part in the landings on Walcheren in Holland. By October 1944, all the Islands surrounding the Scheldt estuary were clear of German control, except for Walcheren Island which was defended as if the outcome of the whole war was in the balance. Its coastal batteries controlled the approach to the Scheldt waterways. Bad weather made air support impossible so the softening up before the landing was done by a Navy bombardment.

The bombardment started from three large battleships of the Royal Navy, HMS *Warspite*, HMS *Roberts*, and HMS *Erebus*. The latter had one inoperable gun turret from damage sustained at Normandy. The West Kapelle battery returned the fire from its battlements. We were initially the inshore defence before taking part in the actual landing. We were stationed between the warships and the Walcheren battlements. During the operation, the bombardment of the coastline at Flushing, you could see these black objects fly overhead as twelve-foot shells, weighing three quarters of a ton, ventured to the shore and arrived in a mass of explosion and debris, leaving only fire in its wake. The sound was like railway trains thundering past as these great shells went back and forth in both directions. It was said that the Resistance movement were hiding in a windmill, which you could see on the coast. When the bombardment was over, all the buildings had been knocked down, pounded, and you could even see a liner which was being built on the slipway, hidden by buildings before the bombardment. Everything was afire, or flattened, but there, standing alone was the windmill, as if a symbol to the accuracy of the British fire, a warning to the German defence of the pending allied dominance and futility of resistance for the landing to come. If it were a message, it was to go unheeded. As the weather cleared, we saw a small number of enemy aircraft and could watch, and even enjoy, them being chased by our fighters,

Tempests or Typhoons. By that stage of the war the allies were pretty much in control of the airways over Europe and so, with a certain degree of bravado and straight out confidence, we made ready for the landing.

The fight for Walcheren and the landing was to be a battle of ferocious intensity. As we landed amidst its deafening sounds of explosions, piercing flashes of tracer fire and the glowing red of our guns, I was hit in the back by shrapnel. A small splinter of metal hit my spinal cord, which, when removed by a medic, did little damage. Another small prayer of thanks and I was soon back on duty. Many years later, another piece of shrapnel, which was missed, was removed from my thyroid gland, and you wonder if the remnants of war will ever leave.

It is difficult to bring to life or give true feeling to any battle and so, for Walcheren, I turn to the *London Daily Mirror,* November 1944, in an article called 'Little Ships Tackled the Shore Guns', which gives a short, but powerful account of the fight:

> *Running unflinchingly and directly into the fire of the mighty German shore batteries on Walcheren Island, small thin hulled British amphibious support vessels fought a battle the like of which sailors who were at Dieppe or Normandy had never seen before.*
>
> *There were heavy losses. The little ships kept their guns hot until they went down or were forced to retire with holes in their sides and bleeding men on their decks. Men on ships, gunboats, rocket ships, and other small craft had been told to engage at point blank range, and knock out if possible, the fixed German gun emplacements lining the dykes and high*

ground near West Kapelle on the Western side of the Island. They went in with all their guns firing, troop laden craft went up behind them to discharge their loads.

With our ships some thousand yards from shore the German guns opened up, suddenly fire belched aboard one, she swung around in the water, another got a direct hit, another raced into the shore with all her guns firing, and turned out again with a single officer left on her bridge and holes in her side.

One gunboat went into the shore, was hit, floundered, and made a last burst to the shore.

The Headquartership LCH 269 was nearly blown out of the water three times, it was a fight lasting nearly five hours.

During the fight, shells bounced off many of the five and six-foot-thick German gun emplacements without effect, until the Commandos were landed, and cut open the gun emplacements with flame throwers and grenades.

Not all engagements are memorable for life lost or their intense ferocity. Another time we were going up the Scheldt, not long after the landings. We thought the Germans had just about been wiped out by bombing. Suddenly heavy guns opened-up from the shore. The first thing we saw were plumes of water coming towards us, then you could see the smoke from the guns and hear the sound; everything was in reverse. Shells arrived first, plumes went up and then you heard the gunfire – BOOM! It all seemed completely in the wrong order. I was leading hand on duty on the bridge and the CO kept quiet while the lookout, pointing to the plumes, stuttered, "Ger-ger-ger," but nothing came out.

So, the CO turned and said to the First Lieutenant, "Is there anything to report, First Lieutenant?"

And the first lieutenant said to me, "Leading Hand of the watch, is there anything to report?"

I said, "Lookout, is there anything to report?"

And he said, "Ger-ger-ger-guns!"

Once we got his "guns" out, the CO pressed the action stations button and said, "Hard a starboard, full ahead" and we moved out of harm's way.

One night, while out on patrol, we unexpectedly came across an enemy minesweeper, an R-boat I believe and, with one burst of fire, it hit our fuel tanks amidships. The same man who stuttered on the bridge, seeing flames pouring out of the fuel hatch and knowing that we only had seconds before the three-thousand-ton tank blew up taking us all with it, picked up a fire extinguisher filled with foam, turned it on, pointed it down the hatch and fought the flames. After the flames were controlled, he pushed the hatch back and, burning hot as it was, locked it in position, turned the fire extinguisher over himself and the hatch, and the fire was out. It was an amazing act of heroism but he received no mention, no recognition. He saved one of His Majesty's ships and its entire crew. You talk to many people, who received Distinguished Service medals or are 'Mentioned in Despatches' and they often say the medal or recognition was for something not as remarkable as other things they were involved with. Our stuttering man saved a ship and its crew, but like countless others in conflict, remains an unknown hero.

It was now December 1944 and the next time we were to go out was just before Christmas - two Sundays before Christmas and another fateful Sunday. Sailing into the minefield as was normal, we left the other three ships that were sailing with us as part of our patrol group, each one going to its own appointed place. We were second in the patrol line and went out to listen for any possible enemy vessels which we would then attack. This patrol had taken us right up the Dutch coast, not far off Ijmuiden in Holland. We were slowly and quietly moving forward and it was my turn on the bridge, listening intensely in the dark and stillness of the night.

After I was relieved, leaving the bridge, I remember walking down toward the aft of the ship, although why I was going there I can't remember. First a clank! And then the bang! We must have hit a mine. For some reason or other, my knees were bent at the time of the explosion, whether I was about to climb up or go down a hatch, I don't know, but I remember being thrown violently forward. My world was in complete silence. I could see several people standing, as though they were at attention, but the force of the explosion had broken their backs and they were dead. How I saw them, I don't know as it was a very dark night. Perhaps the explosion had temporarily lit up the night.

I was brought back to my senses – the temporary silence broken - when hearing the first lieutenant's voice calling me to the bridge. That momentary void which followed the explosion was replaced by all the noises of a ship and men in distress. I made my way to the bridge and the CO spoke to me while thrusting a torch into my hands. I could hear one of the officers calling out, "Hands to Abandon Ship stations, starboard side," Those living or able made their way to the starboard side of the ship.

The skipper said to me, "Inspect all hatches going down the port side of the ship, round to the starboard, and I'll meet you at the

Abandon Ship position. See and report on any casualties or anybody you see. Shout if you need any help."

I made my way from the bridge to start my search. Shining my torch down into the forward mess deck hatch, I was surprised to see that there was water halfway up the gangway. We were sinking fast and luckily there was obviously nobody there. I made my way to the engine room hatch. Lifting the hatch, I was met by the awful sight of the motor mechanic, who was terribly mutilated, dead, and one other person whom I was unable to identify. It would have been one of the engine room staff, one of the stokers, dead. I made a mental note and was about to resume my search when I saw something out of place and unexpected, which for a second, masked the adrenaline and a wave of sadness swept through me. There can be nothing sadder than a human being killed, but there was the ship's pet cat, floating dead on the top of the water. I made my way down to the wardroom aft, but couldn't get down the hatch. Already, the water was coming over the deck of the ship. Since I knew where all three officers were, I presumed there would be nobody else there, so I made my way to the Abandon Ship station.

I was wearing my life-jacket, as we all were, and had in my pocket an inflatable life-belt. I was putting that round my neck when the captain asked for a report and I told him what I had seen. The order was for the three of us to remain fast, including the captain; for the other crew the order was given, "Two paces, forward march." They went one step and before the second stride could be completed, splash they were in the water. This was December, mid-winter in the North Sea, with a water temperature of about six degrees Celsius. Life expectancy in those conditions would be short.

The captain asked that I go around and check for a final time. He did not give a reason nor did I ask, but a captain would not want to leave an injured person onboard to drown while the crew abandoned ship. Even when all hands were accounted for, you still had to be vigilant. Towards the latter part of the war, sometimes shore-based staff used to stow away just for the sake of a trip. It was strictly taboo, but I believe it was even known to occur in aircraft. A plane would go up, only to find one extra on board.

We went around one more time, and this time, I was caught up by the captain. We moved to the engine room hatch where he looked down, strangely enough, this time we couldn't see the bodies in the engine room from the hatch. But as the numbers were agreed upon, those bodies would be left to go down with the ship. When we came to the ship's side, even in that gloom and dark, it was obvious that the people in the water could see us and several were shouting something like, "Don't go over there! Don't go over there!"

I couldn't quite work out what they were saying. Was it "Oil on the water!?" They were still calling out when the coxswain stepped into the water and the CO and I followed. Striding out into the dark and into freezing water is an experience that must be lived to be believed. On a cold winter's night, imagine jumping naked out of a window into the nearest river. Your life jacket comes up from underneath and nearly pulls your neck off as you hit the water. You sink briefly before the buoyancy of the jacket wrenches you to the surface. The cold is so intense and the shock so immediate that your body thinks its dying and then suddenly, your eyes are hurting and you're struggling for breath. I was breathing and swallowing oil instead of air. Everything tastes of oil. It's burning. Your skin is on fire. The more delicate parts of you are in absolute agony from the cold. The pain is unbelievable as the petrol, oil and cold bite deeply into your soul and you recognise that death would not be an unfriendly thing.

Then unexpectedly, you can breathe, but only just. Your mouth is above the oil and you strike out in some direction or the other, and suddenly - Yes, you're free of the oil and you cry out, but nothing comes out. Then you are sick, vomiting, retching. As anyone who has been violently bilious knows, at the time you really don't care if you live or not. The pain. I couldn't open my eyes. I couldn't see. I must have been going blind from the petrol in my eyes. The excruciating pain. You try and move your hand, but you can't feel it. *"It's not so cold, it's not so cold, it's not that bad,"* you tell your mind as it plays with you in a kaleidoscope of cascading and contradictory thoughts. *"I feel free, I'm okay. Yes, I have undone my shoes. Don't get pulled down into the sea. Remember your drill from those first days of training, naked in the submarine training tank: keep talking to yourself, keep warm, and don't give in. Where is everybody? Is there anybody around? I must call out."* Yes, I can speak now, but when I try and call out, I'm sick again - so terribly sick. Time, your mortal enemy, moves at an indistinguishable pace, accompanied by confusion, its surreptitious friend. The water is so cold, it's up your nose and in your mouth, making it difficult to breathe, and still the stench of petrol and oil makes you vomit again. I pass out, awakening confused, *"Where am I? Is there anybody there? It's so dark. Nobody. Nothing. I'm alone."*

I still couldn't see and my eyes burned from the oil. *"How long will this go on?"* Am I now inviting death? *"Am I going to die?"* The memory of old Jock returned. This was another Sunday evening: "Would they be praying for us now?" Perhaps, he was right. This is ridiculous. *"Where's my God now?"* Will the sea be my Calvary? For the first time, I had a feeling that I knew what it was like to be on the cross. *"Why, dear God, why now, after all I've been through? Why save me only to let me die now? Why?"* Was it wrong - pure arrogance to yell out the words, *"My God, My God, why hast thou forsaken me?"* The cold, the pain, but I must live. I want to live.

The sea that night was still. It did not strike in turbulent anger but remained remarkably calm, instead taking its vengeance with tentacles of cold that ripped at the remnants of human dignity. I was shivering now, really shivering, as hypothermia found its reluctant companion. Your consciousness is aroused as something bumps into you and you think, *"That might be a mine."* You don't think of sharks in the North Sea. *"If it is a mine, it could explode,"* but why be frightened of a mine exploding? It would bring peace by stealing away your agony; perhaps, it already did and I am already dead. You force your eyes open, and the burning begins to ease as the petrol slowly evaporates from them. I was sick again and this time remembered not being able to breathe because of the violent retching. I was vomiting out both my mouth and nose.

That bitter enemy, the cold, had by now, begun to depart. I remember saying to myself, *"I don't feel all that cold,"* but fear prevailed with the memory that when you were suffering thermal loss, although I don't think we knew the word 'thermal loss' back then, it was said you began to feel warmer. If I wanted to live, it would now be a battle of the mind. I remember thinking, *"I've got to start talking. I've got to start speaking and, if I speak, somebody might hear me."* I physically felt a little better now, as I must have vomited out most of the oil that I had swallowed. As the battled raged within my mind, I suddenly had this overwhelming feeling of the depth and vastness of water under me. There were these little bits of wood floating nearby on the water. Even in the dark, I could see them and I reached out, trying to catch one, to touch something solid with my hand, but I couldn't.

It was still dark, but I remember looking up and seeing the sky quite light. I thought dawn must be breaking, but how could I have been in the water so long? Looking again, it was a light up there. I could see a light, then the pain, the tremendous pain, returned. I felt as though I was being skinned and the flesh was being ripped from my body. Where are the other people? *"Oh God, why me?"* In the Psalms, they argue: Where are you now, God? Why have you done this to us? When will you hear us? I had always believed in God, but did I now doubt? Would God answer my prayers? Or would he watch, in loving compassion, as I moved towards the light? I didn't know my scripture well then, but I remember thinking of a Bible passage where somebody challenges God and says, "Now God, will you change your mind if....." Why shouldn't I argue and challenge God? Why shouldn't I say, "Why have you done this? Why me?" Why shouldn't I bargain? "God, if you get me out of this, I'll do anything you want of me. You saved my life on the Atlantic convoys. You saved me on the landing at Walcheren. God, maybe there is a job for me to do. If I am saved, then my life no longer belongs to me. If I am saved, my life will belong to you. My life will be one of service, of doing things for others. *"Can you hear me, God?"*

Time itself had slowed, ceasing its relentless and persistent march forward. Seconds had become hours and minutes an eternity. It was unbearable and I was slowly losing the battle with my mind. Torrents of bleak thoughts once again, began to overwhelm me. *"Have I been here minutes or hours or even days?"* I was disoriented. *"I can see a ship, it's very tall and it's a big ship."* I tried to call out, but I had no voice, not even a whisper; nothing. I tried again with all the energy I had left to call out but became violently sick; more vomit, more oil and now blood. I knew the taste as I had sipped it once before, when poor old Jock got blown to pieces.

I can see a ship, its lights. I can see the numbers *243*. *"Am I hallucinating?"* That's the ship I came off – *243*. It's just lying there. It hadn't sunk and was high enough out of the water for its number to be showing.

I can hear voices. Somebody is shouting. *"I've got to shout back. I'm so tired. I don't care. Am I dreaming? Am I hallucinating?"* My eyes are closed, it's so painful. Somebody is putting a rope around me, under my arms.

"Heave away!" I'm being pulled up.

"Is he dead?"

"Think so." *"Yes, I'm dead, so this is what it's like to be dead. Ooh bang! That hurts and I must have made a sound.*

"Ah! You're aloive." It's the Coxswain's voice.

The CO was in the water with me and the coxswain was pulling me up.

I was now on the deck. "Who is it?" I heard someone say said as they looked at me. At that time, they didn't recognise who I was or perhaps, what I was.

Then suddenly, somebody said, "For God's sake, get him warm!" and I was dragged. I am sure I was dragged because I remember bouncing over things and being lifted into the deckhouse, and then into the wheelhouse.

"Now don't take his clothes off, it'll be warmer with this. Like us, he's covered in oil. Leave it caked on. That will keep the heat in. Massage his feet and hands, we don't want him to lose them."

Gradually, my senses began to come back.

"It's Biggs, one of the last three to go over! Where are the remainder? Get out and start looking for them."

I lay there in bad shape and, when I eventually came to, I learned that I was asleep, or out of it, for about one and a half hours. They thought at one time I had slipped away, but I was still there. Then there was a vibrating sound; engines ... E boats ... enemy E boats.

The CO called the coxswain and me to action stations. An easy target though we were, *243* was not going down again without a fight. Did the Oerlikons (cannons) go under? I found myself moving up to a cannon as the sound of the boat got closer. Positioning myself behind the guns, the cannon was cocked, ready to fire. Would she fire? Then I could see other ships coming. It was one of ours, the flotilla leader. For that simple action, the actions of that night, where we were willing to fight despite the futility of our position and for what we would do over the next few days, the ship was later awarded the Distinguished Service Cross (DSC) and the Distinguished Service Medal (DSM). The skipper was awarded the DSC, the coxswain and I dug in the hat for the DSM, the coxswain pulled the DSM, and I received a Mentioned in Despatches (MiD).

This would be the night that marked the beginning of my journey to God, and along with it - a lifelong promise to keep.

Even to this day, I'm still not one hundred percent sure what happened. As best I can determine, following the explosion and as the ship sank, it appeared that the engines fell out of the bottom of the ship. Being made of wood, she somehow then floated back up. You would have thought the engines would have caused a larger hole as they crashed through the bottom of the ship and caused her to sink faster. But with the engines gone, she popped up and the three of us would live.

We were taken in tow by the flotilla leader and all three of us, one lieutenant and two leading seamen, acting as one, decided that we weren't going to leave the ship. "Then I'll have to drag you to the enemy coast," the leader had said.

While in tow, we suddenly remembered that we hadn't got rid of important papers. Charts, papers and all things that could not fall into enemy hands were gathered together. I remember watching because I wasn't yet strong enough to provide much assistance. I just rested. The papers and other secretive belongings were weighted and thrown over the side. After a while, I felt fit enough to stand on the wheel even though she didn't answer the helm as there was nothing there. It was a symbolic but none-the-less an important gestor.

As we approached the enemy beach, the flotilla leader came alongside and we were given all sorts of warm clothing, tins of food, hot drinks and other supplies. Along with the necessities was about two week's supply of rum which proved to be very difficult to open. They forgot that you must break the seal on the top of Pussers Navy rum. I never did have a taste for alcohol, but like smoking, which was introduced to me while on the convoys, I learned to enjoy a tot of rum from then on. It kept you warm and it really did possess medicinal properties; pain, of all types, always seemed to subside – that my story and I am sticking to it.

With a sudden burst of speed, like a sling shot, we were launched towards the shore but before we could cut the umbilical cord, the cast-off line, which had tethered us to the tow ship, broke. I remember the sound of the line going "Boing!" I can still hear that note. The momentum given to us from our tow ship however was already enough and we powered on. Then, with a sudden crunching sound, we found the beach. We were swung round by the waves before eventually settling high and dry. At last we were on dry land yet beached in enemy territory. It must have been dead on high tide when we found our new, temporary but welcome home.

So, we had arrived in Holland, beached and in our damaged MTB. Did we have a plan? If this story were being told by the CO, the answer may well be "Yes." His story would tell of plans made with the flotilla leader for the beaching, repair and recovery of both the ship and us. But this is a story as seen through the eyes of an ordinary sailor and who was, at the time, just twenty-one years of age. Such plans, if they were made, were not shared. So, for me, looking back in retrospect, it appears fate was to be allowed to play out her game of chance. I doubt at the time that I even questioned what was to happen. Ah – to be British.

We slept, but couldn't wash as we were terribly short of fresh water, but we did have beer. I drank my first can of beer and I think it was the first one, canned beer that is, I had ever seen. It must have come from the ward room. The beer looked rather like cans of Brasso in those days, with a screw metal top.

I had recovered sufficiently to keep things down so anything, food or drink was both good and necessary. There was however some discomfort, pain after I ate, even if only a little in comparison to being in the sea.

Night had become day and here we were, a British MTB, high and dry on a beach, somewhere in Holland. In the distance, we could hear the hum as a plane, an ME109G, flew along the coast. It was only then that we noticed the white star of the allied forces on our ship, blazing for all to see. As beautiful as the star was, it was probably not a good look for a crew marooned on an enemy beach and needed to be quickly covered. Searching for any stuff that may help in obscuring our beacon, we made our way to the front hatch, and found, believe it or not, paint and paintbrushes. With the material at hand, we set about creating our disguise, even if it only amounted to painting over the star. A little later, another ME hummed into view and flew over, this time coming quite low as if to look. Obviously satisfied, it dipped its wings, one side and then the other; a hello or welcome from the skies. We all waved and she flew gracefully on, disappearing slowly into the distance. It would not take long before we were discovered. The only question was, by which forces, allied or German?

I give a slight chuckle and opening my eyes momentarily while still thinking back to that time. Then once more I allow the memories of the past to fill my dreams. Here we were, sitting on our boat, stranded in enemy territory not far from Ijmuiden. In my dream, I can see daylight giving leisurely way to evening. All is quiet, silence broken only by the gentle lapping of the sea as it kissed the shore. In what was to be one of those rare and surreal experiences, even with the passing of time the memories never fade. Far off into the distance, we heard people singing. Christmas carols: 'Hallagen Nacht,' 'Silent Night' in German providing a tranquil harmony to the symphony of the sea. With the beautiful German singing penetrating the stillness of the evening, we suddenly heard the movement of people near our boat, and then, in a most beautiful Oxford accent, someone said, "Army here" as they clambered aboard our ship.

The Army brought canvas, which we put over the hole in the bottom of the ship. Only then did we begin to see what a mess the ship was in. It appears the whole bottom of the ship was missing. Then, as if by magic, more people arrived, carpenters and engineers, and with a flurry of hammering and trades people stuff, the bottom of the ship was sealed. Now with our ship's makeshift repairs complete, the Army officers suggested that we be taken to hospital even if just for a check-up, but the CO said, "We're staying with the ship," and with that, the salvage crew vanished from whence they came.

Without a tow, *243* would have to remain beached - unable to extract herself from the grip of Terra Firma. We would need to await a high tide and a rescue craft. With nothing more to do we stayed on the beach all the next day, which proved very uneventful. You would think that a small warship, sitting on the beach, would attract the attention of somebody, friend or foe, but it didn't. After the Army left we just sat there an insignificant piece of drift wood, a mosaic in the complex theatre of war.

The next night, a ship of considerable size, most likely a Bims Minesweeper, arrived at high tide to tow us off and take us home. *243,* at least initially, was unwilling to return to the sea. We broke two or three tow lines and then finally, with two cables attached, one of which snapped, flying back at colossal speed and striking the ship with such force you thought the ship would be cut in half, we came free of the beach and were once again afloat. The repairs of our Indefatigable held, at least they were not letting the water in faster than the several deck pumps, which had by now been installed, could manage. With the lines attached and our confidence high, we began the slow and tentative return trip, home to England.

The crew from the towing ship provided us with water, food and more clothing, while beseeching us to leave the ship, but again, our CO refused. We were not going to abandon our ship again so we were towed, on what was for us, an enormous journey back across the Channel to Britain. With the pumps running at full speed, they struggled to keep pace with the relentless sea and we had to keep a close watch on the water levels as the battle for buoyancy raged. But the sea, that winter's night, was as calm as I have ever seen it and, as we sliced through its glassy surface, the pumps in compact with the sea, an accord written in heaven, afforded a fighting chance to bring our ship safely home.

With Poseidon sleeping and Anemoi at rest, after a passage of time of which I cannot remember, perhaps two days, we entered the Thames estuary and were unceremoniously dragged to Ramsgate. Toward the final part of our journey, *243* had become tired, she was broken and, despite her resolve, she was not going to return home easily. The pumps and repairs were falling short of the challenge and water was on the rise. But with home in sight, the Navy rallied and more people and pumps were brought on board. The ship was not to be lost, so with everybody helping, just after dusk, we finally made it to Ramsgate. The boom gates which were normally up by that hour had been left down in anticipation of our return.

We were home. What followed became one of the proudest moments of my life. At the beginning, as I thought about my story, I said things about senior officers - now I take them back. Standing on Ramsgate dock, waiting for us, was the Admiral of Nore, the Commander in Chief (CNC). As we were helped, in our now rather dishevelled condition onto the dockyard, the admiral came forward and saluted. "Well done, gentlemen," he said. "Take these men immediately to hospital," and instructed that we were to be taken in his personal car. But before we were placed in his car, he turned to the two of us, the non-officers. We, of course, had no hats on and he said, "You, as leading seamen, would know that you never salute without a hat on." "Yes, sir," we replied and he gave us a salute we were unable to return; this was recognition from the Navy.

Although thankful to be home, your mind can never wander far from those who did not return.

Chapter Thirteen
Meaning of Life

I spent a very short time in hospital as my recovery was quick. The privilege, or is it, the perils of youth? I was sent on a short shore leave and, returning home, I kept my secret promise never to burden my parents with any misadventures the war might bring. Mother was an intuitive woman and noticed that I had lost my watch and some of my clothing was missing, although my clothing since the beginning of the war was never quite right. Even at the war's end, I never told my parents of that Sunday night, shortly before Christmas, not far from Holland. I told them that we lost a propeller shaft and had to be towed home. I was already a church-going man so Christmas was already an important celebration but, from that moment on, Christmas took on a greater, more joyful significance. In Church, as we sang 'Silent Night' and celebrated the birth of Jesus, I thanked the Lord for my life which was not taken that night.

I was re-kitted and moved from one *243* to another *243*. I served on both an MTB *243* and an ML *243* which caused some confusion in mail delivery and then, later, my war record. Now on ML *243* it was back to familiar duty where we spent quite a bit of time transporting what seemed to be important people from the continent to England. It was now close to the end of the war in Europe. Our patrols almost inevitably had us back in England on Thursday, so I could join the local church youth group, with my promise to God never too far from my mind.

With the end of hostilities in May 1945, I transferred to MTB *5003* and was to remain at sea in one capacity or the other, minesweeping and other operations, until the summer of 1946, when I was demobilised. I loved the sea and boats and still do, but after 1946, I never even stepped into a rowboat, let alone swam in the sea. I wasn't psychologically affected, but the war had influenced me in many ways and continued to do so right up to my very last moments.

War takes so much from, and of, a person. You re-enter civilian life empty, a void waiting to be filled. How that space is filled is the important question for a future after war. If you don't choose, the past has a habit of choosing for you. Because I survived, I was determined that the influences, the touch of war, should be motivating, positive and give meaning to my future life.

I never forgot the promise I made to God that night as I floated in the North Sea, *"If I am saved, my life will belong to you."* It would take until my midlife before I finally fulfilled that pledge. On Monday 25th July 1966, I was made Deacon by Kenneth Lord, Bishop of Lincoln and ordained a Priest on Sunday 21st May 1967 by the same Kenneth Lord in the Cathedral Church of St. Mary. My journey as a Priest began in Cornwall as a Curate in the Parish of Truro.

Britain took a long time to recover from war and even in the late 1960s, things were tough. Australia in those days, unlike now, wanted migrants (if they were white - Australia had the 'White Australia Policy'). Its call seemed to entice, an offer of a new life, a new beginning, a better future. It was, as I am sure it still is, a momentous decision to leave the country of your birth. To leave your family and friends with the intention of making a new life thousands of miles away. The decision was difficult enough but at least we spoke the language. What must it be like for many who, for whatever reason, leave their homes, for a place whose language and culture is foreign? I was lucky and with a great friend in Australia, Bert Neil, I was offered my first parish, Loch/Poowong, by the then Bishop of Gippsland, David Arthur Garnsey.

The letter we received from the Chief Migration Officer - Office of the High Commissioner for Australia, reflects the times. It seems almost humorous now, but then it mirrored our dreams for a better future in Australia, which for us came true.

> *Dear Rev. Bigge:* (should have read Biggs)
>
> *Now that your arrangements for migration are complete, I should like to wish you a happy journey and every success in your new life in Australia.*
>
> *We Australians are proud of our country and hope that you too may soon be proud to call it your own.*
>
> *It is a young, vigorous country, very much bigger than Britain and different in many ways. You will nevertheless find much in Australia to remind you of "Home" as Australians call Britain, for Australia was founded and build by Britons and upholds firmly her British heritage and loyalties.*
>
> *You may miss some of the things familiar to you but you will discover in Australia many advantages that Britain lacks, particularly for your children's future. The many thousands of Britons who have gone before you have found that opportunity and happiness are there for those who work for them………*
>
> *Yours sincerely,*
>
> *R.E. Armstrong, CHIEF MIGRATION OFFICER*

Moving to Australia, we left Britain on the 30th June 1970 from Gatwick Airport on flight QF110 and flew to Sydney as £10 Poms, meaning you paid £10 and the Australian government paid the rest (£20 by the time we came, which included our train fares to the airport). Most of what we had, which was not much, our worldly belongings, were shipped by Blatchfords Packers and Removers for the grand total of £230.60; not a lot of money even by the standards of the day. We had used most of our savings, including the sale of the house to pay for my theological training and, like many before us from all over Europe, we left Britain with very little for a new beginning, a better life in Australia. From the moment we arrived in Australia it was our home and we were to never have even a fleeting thought of returning to Britain.

The rest of my life was to be in service to the church, first in the parish of Loch/Poowong and then Drouin; both in Victoria, Australia. I was to retire to a beautiful little hamlet call Brandy Creek, not far from Drouin.

Like my Navy service, my religious career was as an ordinary parish priest, never climbing the hierarchy of the church. Along with my regular parish responsibilities, I was a prison chaplain on French Island, the prison now long since closed, and a marriage guidance officer. But it was the work I did in mental health, for which, in 2003, I would receive the Centenary Medal, that brought me the greatest satisfaction. Like one in five families, we were touched by mental illness when one of my children, from a very young age, began a lifelong struggle with schizophrenia. My wife and I assisted in the development of support groups and programmes for people with mental illness. For thirty years, I volunteered on committees, worked with the Department of Human Services and, at times, spoke at universities and on television about issues surrounding mental health and the impact on families. Perhaps, if war taught me the value of life, schizophrenia taught me the value of one's own mental health and spiritual well-being.

It is possible that the seeds for joining the ministry were sown long before that fateful night in the North Sea, as I had always had a strong interest in the church. You do wonder, at times, if the series of events, the rich tapestry of what is life, is just a guide taking us down a path that we were always destined to travel. Perhaps then I was always going to become a Priest. It would however be that night in the sea that resonates for me as the turning point. After that night, I knew that there was something greater than all of us and that life was meant for more than just existing. There is, above and beyond us all, a greater power and a responsibility that we each hold to one another. No matter the demands of life, its stresses and strains, even if we experience great tragedy and loss, we have a duty to use our experiences for the good of others. But for those of us who are fortunate enough to be spared, whether touched by fate or by the hand of God, we have a duty greater than most to give and share that time, which might not have been ours, for the betterment of others. Whether you believe in God or not, as you look out and marvel at what is the miracle and beauty of life on this earth, or peer up into the night sky in amazement, you cannot help but contemplate and be touched by an overwhelming sense of our own insignificance. There must be something more, something greater than us.

As I sit here thinking about my story, I musingly wonder if the desire for a life in service was not, in part, a reflection of living with the guilt of surviving. My story like many ordinary people in times of war, is remarkable, but remarkable not for what I did, but that I am here and able to tell my story. Even now, I can't pretend to understand why, every day all over the world, some people live while others die. What I do know however, is that I am grateful for having lived a long and happy life and, whether because of my experiences, guilt or a true belief in doing good, I have tried to never take for granted the time, which perhaps, was not mine to be had.

My life as a church minister, its happenings and the stories, are far more fascinating than the war. There is something grand in being seen by many as a bumbling old vicar, for often you become the safety deposit box, either purposely or inadvertently, for what some may call their secrets. But it is the people, their politics and the church itself that could fill many volumes. Some stories are not as charitable or Christian in form as one might want or expect. Unfortunately, in many ways the politics of the church could rival any parliament. It is not difficult then to appreciate why some see the church as hypocritical, particularly when you see how so called Christians can treat each other, let alone those outside the church. Our righteous beliefs all too frequently pass judgements on other - a judgement not ours to give. Our papers have in recent times been filled with the stories of 'Men of God' using the church as a façade to perpetrate against children, to fulfil their deviant sexual and immoral desires. The institution which is the church has too often cared more about itself than the needs and welfare of the abused. It is not difficult to see why there is a crisis of confidence in religion in general and the church specifically.

The war was to provide a valuable training ground for life in the church and in particular, the hand-to-hand combat that I learned and later taught. One evening, when I was well into my sixties, I was on my nightly stroll. I think because of the war, where most of our missions and activities were done in the dark, I found solitude in peace time by walking late at night, in the safety of the dark. I saw a flash of light bouncing across the inside of the windows of the church which was, otherwise, in pitch darkness. These occasional flares of light, appearing and then swiftly disappearing, suggested someone was inside. I made haste to confront whatever intruders I might find and, bursting through the front door, I moved deftly towards the inner double swing doors. Pushing open one side of the inner doors, I felt the breeze as a fist whistled inches from my face, but it failed to find its mark. Forty years may have passed since the combat training and what happened next, I cannot fully recall, but the owner of the fist lay in a heap, moaning on the carpet in front of me. Another assailant burst past, making all speed to exit the church and quite intent on leaving his accomplice stranded and prostrate behind. I turned and this short, bald, chubby, sixty-something clergyman, in full flight, gave chase to a gazelle-like teenager. Some distance up the road I finally admitted defeat as the gazelle accelerated away and vanished into the distance. Returning to the church, by now some twenty minutes later, I fortunately discovered that the other young man had vanished. I imagined that he was sore but otherwise unharmed from the experience.

When I was well into my seventies, I returned to my car which was parked in Warragul, a town not far from Drouin, only to find the driver side door open and a young man kneeling with his hands under the dashboard, attempting to hotwire the car. I was overwhelmed by a flash of intense rage and for a few brief seconds any weariness of age dissolved. I delivered a short and powerful kick. The thief's head and body joined his hands under the dash. Reaching inside the car, I pulled the young man out and pushed him into the gutter. Taking my keys from my pocket, I gently I lowered my old body into the driver's seat, started the car and reversed out into the street and drove home. When I returned home, my family were mortified as I recounted the events. There was no concern for the attempted theft of my car. Rather, that I couldn't go around beating people up, let alone, pushing them into the gutter and driving off! Although they wanted me to go to the police, I was happy to wait, confident the police would find me if they wanted me. If they did, perhaps, the story would make the 'Odd Spot' in the Age newspaper: 'Seventy-five-year-old priest beats up car thief!'

Although an Anglican, my family would describe me as being more Catholic than the Pope. I liked the old traditions and rituals of church services, singing evensong, the choirs, the *bells and smells*' as some would call it and, the more incense, the better. That's not to say we didn't, at times, have modern and youth services, for we did. The late 1970s and 1980s was a time of congregational growth in the Gippsland diocese. The diocese had a very active group of young people called the Gippsland Young Anglicans, many of whom came from my parish of Drouin, and it was not uncommon for the Rectory to be filled with young people. If all my services had been 'bells and smells', there would have been a revolution! But where I found my comfort was in the old rituals. I was an old traditionalist so I always wore black trousers, a black shirt with a white dog collar and, although not intended, I blended nicely on my evening walks into the dark of the night.

Toward the latter part of my life, I was to be touched by two events which were to reshape my faith.

The first would test my understanding of what it means to be a Christian but, at the same time, it provided a greater clarity and comfort in those twilight years as I prepared to leave this world in death. From an early age, I had what I thought was a good understanding of what it meant to be a Christian and this understanding developed and grew as I matured, but that's not to say, even as a minister, that I didn't have times of doubt. It was this acceptance of what it is to be Christian, which was about to be challenged by the first of these two experiences.

While undergoing an operation, I temporarily died and, like many have seen in the movies or read, I floated above, looking down upon my body, listening and watching as the medical staff worked frantically. Upon my recovery, I recalled to the surgeon conversations and observations known only to those present in the room, which I technically should not have known. During this time, as I floated above my body, there was for me, no light at the end of a tunnel but a sudden and overwhelming revelation, as though a veil of ignorance was lifted and I could now see clearly. I now understood.

In the 1960's and at the height of the Cold War, one of my sons, then eight years of age, asked me where the 'Iron Curtain' was. While the 'Iron Curtain' was a geographic boundary, it was not an actual curtain made of iron. Despite my best efforts, at that stage of his development, he could not comprehend how this could be. Then, perhaps what was two or three years later, he looked up from his dinner and said, "I know. It just happened. I understand what the 'Iron Curtain' is." He had a flash of insight; an 'Aha' moment.

During that near-death experience, I had one of those moments of 'spontaneous comprehension'. I suddenly knew that if you were Muslim, it was the Muslim God who was waiting for you. If you were Christian, it was the Christian God and if you were Jewish, it was the Jewish God. The revelation was, however, greater than the three large Abrahamic religions (Judaism, Christianity and Islam). My discovery was that it made no difference if you were Buddhist, Hindu, or Callathumpian, your God, the God of all mankind was waiting for you. There truly was a greater being and an existence beyond this life on earth, but for all people of all faiths. The experience, at least initially, was a real dilemma for me and would eventually transform my understanding of what it meant to be Christian and to know God. I concluded that

Christianity was not wrong, but it was only one of many ways and paths to God. This revelation did not disappoint me, for Christianity was my path, but it did fill me with a greater sense and understanding of the breadth of God's love and our insignificance in this place. I began to understand, for perhaps the first time, the difference between faith and believing: faith in my Christian life, and believing, or rather knowing, there is one God for all peoples, regardless of their religion or beliefs.

As an ordained minister in the Anglican Church, you may ask, how did I reconcile the discovery that Christianity was not the only path to knowing God? What did this mean for the role and relevance of the Christian church and for my congregations? Had my life and that promise I made to God all been in vain? In the end, my new understanding did not diminish but strengthened my belief in both the church and the importance of congregational membership of the church, each of which are for me, central to both my own and the broader Christian identity. I believe that membership to a church, along with its rites and rituals, can support and nourish. The familiarity of those rites and rituals can provide comfort and certainty in this ever-changing world, but that is not to say that I think the church should remain static. On the contrary, the church must continue to change and evolve if it wishes to maintain its relevance in the modern world. Our understanding of the Bible, and the acceptance that we will never fully understand it, happens within the church, and our Christian identity is formed through the church.

I felt even stronger than before that the church should provide a platform for a collective good and this good should show itself through the behaviour of its people. Through its teachings, the church and its ministers can guide us on the journey of belonging, knowing and behaving as God requires and as famously quoted from the prophet, Micah 6:8:

Micah asked, "What does the Lord require of you?"

He answered, "To do justice, to love kindness, and to walk humbly with your God."

To me, this commanding but simple sentence describes what it is to be Christian and it is through a robust Christian institution like the church that its ministers can nurture our faith and what it means to be Christian. They can also encourage and support us in challenging and discussing the varied social and ethical dilemmas which arise and will continue to arise in this ever-changing world.

I concluded that the type of life you lead, the person you are and the service you give, are the truly important parts of spirituality and living in the shadow of God. These are, in some ways, more important than 'religion', but it is often through religion that we find a voice and community for the way that we should live and behave.

I recovered from the operation and with many years of ministry in front of me, a new and deeper certainty had developed of the varied and many paths to the life after this, and the relevance of the Christian church. As a Christian, I continued to teach the path through the New Testament, but the experience changed for me what it meant to be a Christian. I became not only more aware of grace, but of the intolerance shown by many who claim the certainty of their own faith, an intolerance toward good people, whose major difference is that they don't share the same beliefs. Now more aware, my greatest sadness came as I observed the intolerance done in the name of Jesus Christ.

After my near-death experience, I now felt that in our more recent times, the Bible and Christianity has been hijacked by a noisy group who purport a Biblical literalism. An almost absolute or literal interpretation of the Bible, which is an *exclusive* rather than *inclusive* Christianity. This slant toward literalism does not encourage, and in many ways, hinders the inquiring mind. A phrase such as 'Intelligent Design,' which could have been a beautiful description of the involvement and mystery of a greater being in the making of the universe, including the science of our universe, has come to mean 'creationism'. Intelligent Design could have given meaning to God's role in creating the building blocks of the universe, the science behind it, the Big Bang, the physics that underpins all that is known and not yet discovered, the Higgs boson particle, and those things yet to be found. In many ways, science enhances the wonder of a greater being who sets these complexities in motion. As an engineer before joining the church, God and science have, for me, always gone together. I remember when I first learned the first and second laws of thermodynamics I could not help but be reminded of the greatness of our creator, and as I stare out and try to ponder the infinity of the universe, I am touched by the presence of something beyond all of us.

Unfortunately, Intelligent Design has, for some, come to represent an absolute or literal interpretation of Genesis and the Bible. God made humans, Adam and Eve, in their present form and this all happened about eight thousand years-ago. Even more alarmingly, some now purport that if you don't support this literal view or interpretation, then you cannot be a Christian and by extension, have access to heaven.

Throughout my theological training and in the eyes of most mainstream Christian religious scholars, Genesis and many of the stories in the Bible were never intended to be literal accounts. The trend towards a more fundamentalist approach, a literal understanding of the Bible, whereby if you don't believe certain things you are not a Christian, risks creating a conservative, narrow and unhelpful understanding of what it means to be

Christian. This not only limits the curious mind but more worryingly creates the capacity for some to make and hold judgement over others. Although a conservative, as I liked some of the old church traditions, I was never theologically conservative and following my epiphany I became increasingly disturbed by the growing voice of literalism from any religion.

For Christianity, I found that a fundamentalist or conservative theological approach gave unintended meaning. It gave power to words or sentences that have, in many instances, been removed from context or the intent of the time in which they were written. As with many issues, the 'narcissism of small differences', can be used to polarise people, who then feel compelled to defend their position or ideology. Such absolutes by any group or any religion can only foster intolerance and do not represent the gracious God I know. A God who welcomes all, regardless of religion and beliefs. Unfortunately, the intolerance of religions, and within religions, has a powerful, bleak and regretful past and yet, this intolerance is still used by some to justify that which cannot be justified in the name of a loving God. It is not difficult to find many examples within our own Christian and the Islamic faith - between the Shiite and the Sunni's.

A conservative Christian theology risks marginalising the church from some of the important social and ethical debates of our times, such as genetic engineering, cloning, refugees and climate change to name just a few. By giving voice to a natural selection versus creationist debate they have, for some, allowed a greater Science versus Christianity argument to occur that can only serve to diminish the credibility of most Christians and other God loving peoples who do not share the literal view.

I realise, rather than thinking about my story, I have broken into a sermon. Perhaps this is the reserve of a priest, but depending upon your view, it may be the folly. It is however through sermons that a priest addresses biblical, theological, social and moral issues. I think then, if I were to write my story, I would include my sermons. In many ways, they would provide a transparent window through which a reader could see and understand my thinking and beliefs. The eyes through which I now see the world. Because of this I will, for a moment, continue to explore that window into my soul.

There need not exist a conflict between science and religion. Science does not set out to undermine or diminish the existence or involvement of God. I recently read the aims of the Richard Dawkins (Evolutionist Biologist and atheist) Foundation. Its stated aim was to "Support scientific education and critical thinking to overcome religious fundamentalism, superstition, intolerance and suffering." As a Christian those aims are totally consistent and representative of my own Christian ideals. The Church should, and needs to be, in these rapidly changing times, an important social and ethical commentator whose input can be sought and valued by the wider secular community as both thoughtful and provoking but also, at times, challenging. The capacity to operate within this space is, I fear, diminished when some argue that all Christians believe such things as the world is only 6,000 or is it 8,000 years old? Or, if you pray hard enough you can be cured of cancer or any other ailments and even, if a person dies before their time, it was God's will.

While the relevance of the traditional churches in the broader Christian, spiritual and secular community may be diminishing, the more conservative theology is gaining both traction and influence. A spiritual hunger and the desire to find meaning is central to our wellbeing. Biblical literalism offers certainty in uncertain times, but in doing so, can give rise to rigid belief systems. A powerful psychological desire to belong is created when home groups and modern business practices are used within an Evangelical, Charismatic or Pentecostal environment.

Despite my concerns, it is true that the Evangelical-Charismatic community provides the church with a model of growth. If the more 'traditional' mainstream churches don't adopt some of their strategies, they will be left with both an aging and declining congregation base. It is difficult to argue that the mainstream churches are meeting the needs of their congregations, let alone the communities they serve, when they are, in effect, dying.

The mainstream churches, with what I broadly describe as a more inclusive and secular theology, find themselves facing many of the current and contemporary issues of the broader community they purport to serve. This is and of itself, not a bad thing. Homosexuality is one such issue and is, for the church, a topic of our times, particularly same sex marriage and even homosexual clergy. Although a conservative myself, it is the use of literal biblical truths in abeyance of the grace of God that concerns me in this debate. While I may hold a sense of what gives me personal comfort, it is not up to us to judge and in some instances, demonise. After my near-death experience, I knew that my faith is in an inclusive Christianity and not an exclusive or absolute Christianity.

Once in the North Sea, and in a time soon to come, I would ask God to answer my prayers, to intervene, so that I may live. It's an incongruity encountered by many in those times of despair and then, perhaps in desperation or in faith, we pray and look to God to intervene in our lives. But most of us know that God does not operate simply in that way, yet prayer is essential to the Christian identity. To pray is simply to live our lives in the presence of God. Prayer is conversation with God. The nature of each person's prayerful relationship with God is unique to that person, as unique as any other relationship we might have with another.

Central to our understanding of God as Christians is that God constantly engages in life with us. It is only natural to share every moment we live with the one who walks in every moment with us as friend and companion. Prayer provides an opportunity to reflect on our daily journey in life, to share our thoughts, feelings, fears and joys with God.

This means we may ask God to help us at any time, but especially in times of crisis. Once in the North Sea, when my life was under threat, I asked God to spare me. And that I came through that time means I am thankful to God that I was spared. I can even meaningfully say I believe God spared me.

How this happened I do not know, but that it happened does not necessarily imply that God intervened in a manner that transcended the way God is always engaged in my life. In bargaining with God to grant me my life that day, I was expressing my desire to live and to live for God. Because I lived while so many died, I came to understand I had a greater duty and responsibility to live as God would have me live. I do that to express gratitude for being spared by God. It even makes sense to me to say I was spared by God for that purpose.

The difficult issue to discern in such an instance is whether my being spared was in direct causal relation to my seeking in prayer to be spared. Would I have been spared if I had not prayed to God to spare me? Had I not been spared - would it mean that God had not heard my prayer? Certainly, others who probably did not pray were spared on that day, and it is likely that some who prayed did not survive. Not being able to find a neat resolution of these matters in no way diminishes the strength and hope that came to me through prayerfully sharing that moment in my life with God.

I pray now not because I expect God to answer my every request but as an expression of the relationship in which I continue to share, with God as friend and companion. Prayer is simply the natural expression of that relationship. Like in any good relationship, the conversation in any situation is shaped by the circumstances of that moment. While some situations lead to praise, thankfulness or quietness, that moment in the North Sea led to my request to survive it. How that worked out related as much to the circumstances of the situation as it did to my relationship with God. Whatever was to happen, I knew God was engaged with me in that moment, and that changed the moment for me.

In the end, everything God offers us in life is offered alone by the grace of God, not because we deserve or request it. That is the wonder of God's love for us. In grace, God offers simply to be with us and to uphold us in even the worst of circumstances because God loves us. Prayer is our response to God's love. It is our expression of an intimate, loving relationship.

I believe in prayer, the power of prayer, and the healing effect prayer can have. However, the outcome of any situation is not because God answers some prayers and ignores others. It is always shaped by the circumstances of the moment as well as by the presence of God in the moment. God alone knows what that means in any given moment. It never means that God ignores us.

> *So, do not fear, for I am with you; do not be dismayed, for I am your God. I will strengthen you and help you; I will uphold you with my righteous right hand (Isaiah 41:10).*

I had long since retired when my youngest son, then forty-four years of age and never wed, announced he was to be married. Perhaps one of the greatest joys of being a priest is having the honour of performing the wedding ceremony of your children, a privilege I had not yet experienced for Mark. I had married my two other children.

It was about this time in 2004, when the catalyst for my second prayer to live occurred. My friends from the Special Operations group, those who did not survive the war were becoming regular visitors in my sleep. Their visits were vivid and, unlike my dreams, did not fade with the morning light. They appeared as I remembered them from the war, and together, they told me that my time on earth was coming to an end. My final wish was to live long enough to be able to perform the wedding ceremony, so once again, I prayed to God to live for just a little longer.

For all those around and close to me, I looked well and healthy, but in my heart, I knew my time was coming to an end, and medically, I was having little strokes, which at the time I did not know. I knew only of the lapses and a fog in clarity covering times gone by. Some of my memories were becoming tainted by all the experiences of a lifetime lived, from books, movies, and even the people I had known. Events separated by time became one.

> *"We with little mercy for those aged, 'silly old fool', can't you hear my cry as the splendour, the magnificence of mind slips, remember me not as now but for my life lived. I fear not death for I have seen - the final journey with dignity I wish now to make."*

It was the eve of the wedding when we gathered at the practice ceremony that my growing, but still secret difficulties, were clearly on parade. It was not that I struggled and stumbled with my words and thoughts. It was that I knew and they knew I might 'stuff up' the wedding and I did so much want to get it right. On the 5th March 2005, I performed the wedding ceremony at Christ Church, Drouin. My words, voice and presence were as strong as they had ever been in both intellect and wit; it was to be one of the happiest days in my later life.

Four weeks later, I became very ill and was taken to hospital, leaving my home for what was to be the final time. In my sleep, my friends once again returned and I was taken back to that fateful Sunday shortly before Christmas, stepping out into the freezing water as my body cried out, slipping below the surface, I struggled to breathe as water filled my lungs.

> *"Even though I walk through the valley of the shadow of death, I will fear no evil, for you are with me; your rod and your staff, they comfort me."*

This time, I do not fight, I do not call out to God to let me live, for death is now a welcome visitor. My soul is at peace, yet the body, now distant, shivers, gurgles and gasps as pneumonia becomes a timely companion. I float to the surface. The intense cold is gone and in the darkness, I know that I am not alone. Dawn must be breaking as a light appears upon the horizon. I can hear voices. A line is secured around me and I am hoisted from the sea aboard our Spanish Merchantman.

God in his grace granted me my final prayer and having performed the wedding ceremony, I was to die ten weeks later, on the 16th May 2005, at peace for having fulfilled my promise, and for a life that I was fortunate enough to have when so many perished. Now in the presence of my God, I recall a beautiful spring morning, in Brandy Creek, Australia. The sky is a radiant deep blue and a transcendent almost mystical sound was coming from the birds. I felt at peace with the world. My mind began to wander and like many people touched by war, I asked, "Have I done enough?"

The End

PART 2
The Author's Journey

Chapter Fourteen
In Search of Truth

I wrote *Above and Beyond* based on memoir notes made by my father, the Reverend Laurence Walter Biggs, my recollections of his stories and an interview he gave as part of the 'Australians at War Archive'.

Above and Beyond tells the story of Laurence Biggs' World War Two military service and how those events would shape and influence his journey to a life in service with God. He became, in later life, an ordained minister in the Anglican Church.

While writing *Above and Beyond*, it was not my initial intention to scrutinise the accuracy of the information on which the story was based. The memoir notes were all written many years after the events – events which were likely, a distant memory. Any inaccuracies would be, in many ways, an important part of the story. As the book was built around his core memories it was never intended to be historically or factually accurate. So, although the central themes of the book are based on a biographical account, it is also a tale.

However, as the book developed, discrepancies emerged between his account and the historical data. Discrepancies also emerged between his 'Certificate of Service' and the historical records. My curiosity grew. What was the truth?

Part Two of *Above and Beyond* is the author's search for the truth.

Growing up as a 'PK' (priest's kid), the son of an Anglican Minister, I had, over time, come to understand that my father's decision to leave a high paying engineering career and become a priest, was the fulfilment of a promise made to God during the war. That promise was only part of his story yet it became an integral part of our journey as a family, and undoubtedly influenced the character of our lives. I remember losing the company car and moving from London to a new home at 66 Oxford Street, Cleethorpes so he could study theology and become a priest. It was because of that promise that we would, in 1970, immigrate to Australia.

It would be unfair to describe us as poor, but the life of a minister and the family was frugal. We had, however, a wonderfully grounded childhood and the move to Australia brought with it opportunities not to be found in Britain.

The promise was no secret, but despite its influence on our lives we, like all generations before us, at least initially, showed little interest in our parents' past. Notwithstanding this apathy, we as a family, had come to know that this promise was made during World War Two, shortly before Christmas, in the freezing waters of the North Sea.

As I read his notes and started the slow task of writing his story, I began to appreciate the commanding influence the war had on my father. Not wanting to write a traditional biography – *I was born on ……..and grew up in …. etc.* I attempted to weave a tale, a narrative, around his notes of the Russian Convoys, special operations and that fateful night in the North Sea. His notes were all written some 40 years after the events, so you expect many inaccuracies. It was his story and so when I set out on the journey, it was not my intent to check it for historical accuracies. As I read and then wrote however, my curiosity grew. My life and that of our family had been formed and influenced by World War Two and particularly that promise. It was, in some ways, as much *our story*. I began to speculate, if I peeled back the layers, the mist of those 40 years, what might the real story divulge?

I am not a historian, nor an amateur historian. But what started as curiosity, some light hearted and rudimentary desk top research, quickly revealed incongruities and anomalies and caused a questioning of the truth. At times, I became torn between what I could prove or disprove and, if I could not find the historical evidence to support central parts of the memoirs, whether I should allow this to influence or change the story, his story.

Was my uncertainty due to a fear that some elements of his story were not true, and I would be risking his integrity by printing something that may not be factually correct? Or, was the uncertainty a reflection of my own fear. A fear that my understanding of who my father was may be wrong.

At the end of my search I was left with a genuine mystery and perhaps another story which will remain forever hidden and untold. What follows then is the peeling back of time, as I share the findings, the anomalies. It is my journey.

The biographical tale of Laurence Walter Biggs has been written. It is up to you to reach your own conclusions, whatever they may be.

With the advent of the internet, most Royal Navy World War Two service records, or at least the names of those who served, are available from 'The Royal Navy Service Records National Archives.' If, however, you enter Laurence Walter Biggs or his service number of JX 392442, it comes back with "No Matches Found," meaning electronically at least, he does not exist. Thankfully, we had a hard copy of his service record (Certificate of Service), which was fortunate when so many records held by the National Archives have been lost or destroyed. As the

Certificate of Service was on parchment and not paper, likely it was the original copy given to him on discharge for the Royal Navy. An original copy was no longer held by Navy Command.

The Certificate of Service is the starting place of any investigation. However, after a review of Laurence Biggs' Certificate of Service and the Navy archives, it became clear that the Certificate of Service may contain inaccuracies which, although not uncommon, made the peeling back of the layers, for an amateur at least, more challenging.

The Certificate of Service appears to have his military service commencing on 21 September 1941 (The date looks as if it 'may' have been changed from 1942 to 1941)

The Certificate of Service contains the name of the ships upon which he served and has him starting his Royal Navy service at HMS *Glendower*, a training establishment, on the 21 September 1942. If, however he commenced in 1941, 12 months of his military service was missing. With the passing of time, the apparently simple task of just confirming the commencement date of his military service was proving somewhat challenging. If the Certificate of Service for whatever reason, contained anomalies in something as basic as 'commencement date', what would this mean for the rest of his military record?

With a little luck, I was fortunate enough to find a copy of his War Gratuity and Post War Credit of Wages, also given at discharge. This supported a commencement date of September 1942.

The autobiographical notes recall him sailing on the Russian convoys on HMS *Scylla*. A period of service on HMS *Scylla* also appears on the service record and the dates match the known times that HMS *Scylla* was on Russian Convoy duties. The memoir notes have HMS *Scylla* meeting HMS *King George V* and HMS

Dasher. By correlating those two ships' movements in combination with his HMS *Scylla* service dates, February 1943, to April 1943, they showed that he was most likely on Convoy JW53 to Murmansk and RA53 on the return journey.

Two other pieces of evidence support convoy duties. First, I obtained a copy of the letter he received from the Russian Consulate, awarding him the 40 years of Victory medal in the Great Patriotic War of 1941-1945 and second, the issuing by the British Ministry of Defence (MoD) on 25 September 2013, of the Arctic Star.

In 2013, MoD issued the Arctic Star for those who served on the Russian convoys or their next of kin. An application for the Arctic Star for Laurence Biggs was made by his surviving spouse Patricia Biggs, my mother. As the Arctic Star is not a commemorative medal, eligibility is vigorously determined as outlined in a letter received from the MoD.

> *The assessment of medal claims is a very skilled and time-consuming task involving reference to personal service records recovered from archives. There can be no shortcut to reading these records, as the aim is to ensure that each individual receives the medals to which they are entitled.*

The issuing of the medal confirms that he served on the Russian Convoys. The question then arises as to the accuracy of his recollections. The greater the accuracy, the more comfort you can have in the remaining story.

A chance discovery of his HMS *Scylla* 'Station Card' confirmed his duties while on board ship and they were as described in the memoir notes. Station Cards were issued to every non-commissioned rank in the Royal Navy when serving on board ship. They showed where their mess was and what their duties were. Station Cards were handed in when going ashore and recovered when back onboard.

The memoir notes were a relatively accurate account of convoy JW53 and RA53, but as the recollections were written some considerable time after the war, the two convoys were often confused, as you would expect. The inaccuracies, in this instance, give weight to the authenticity to this part of the story.

Accompanying the MoD application for the Arctic Star medal was a request to obtain/access a copy of the material/references they used to determine entitlement. Unfortunately, we did not even receive an acknowledgement of the request let alone a response other than, that is, the issuing of the medal.

Prior to leaving on convoy duties he was, according to the memoir notes, selected for officer training. He commenced upon his return in April 1943. The Certificate of Service is marked with a stamp which shows that he was selected for officer training. This again indicates that this part of the story is accurate.

The investigation now moved to that part of the war where the autobiographical notes say he joined a *special operations group*; perhaps a continuation of activities he was engaged in prior to the war. These special operations duties occur, according to the story, concurrently while an instructor attached to HMS *Gosling*. As you would anticipate, there is no mention of special operations duties on the Certificate of Service. The records do, however, corroborate the story that, while stationed at HMS *Gosling*, a shore-based training establishment, he was an instructor.

It was from HMS *Gosling,* where he was an instructor that he would secretly leave those duties to participate in covert operations, returning to instructor duties upon the mission's completion. Although the Certificate of Service does not record special operations it may however hint that he had sea time while an instructor. When appointed as an instructor, he was made a Leading Seaman. This, in general, means someone with sea experience however, it is reasonable to assume that the rank may have been given in recognition of instructors' duties. This being the case, the rank is withdrawn on 5th September 1944, after his shore-based duties. However, the rank is reinstated, albeit in an acting capacity, the very next day, 6th September 1944, with his deployment to Coastal Forces and a Motor Torpedo Boat (MTB *243* according to his Certificate of Service). It would seem highly unlikely that a person would be appointed as a leading seaman on a Coastal Forces vessel without recent sea time.

In the autobiographical notes, before starting special operations duties he went to Flint Castle for familiarisation with converted vessels. He names such vessels as the *Gay Viking* and *Gay Corsair*, which provide us with a date of around June to September 1943, which matches his service record. Between five and eight converted gunboats were used by Coastal Forces for special operations. *Gay Viking*, the blockade runner, was the most famous. The boats were notoriously unreliable, which again, supports elements of the story.

The history of the SOE has been well documented however, from his notes of transporting operatives I was unable to identify any of the missions from the available listing of SOE, Secret Intelligence Services (SIS/MI5) or Commando activities, although I found very similar stories. You would also anticipate, like the convoys, some confusion recalling the specifics of the various operations which makes it more challenging to identify individual missions. Although I could not find a record of the missions, it is also unlikely that a description of every special operation was made or, if it was, is still currently available. I recall once a conversation with my father when he met a lady living in Bunyip, Australia, who said she had been involved with SOE. He said they discussed the inaccuracies contained within an authoritative text written about the SOE. This means however that he had read about the various SOE operations during World War Two. Both were in their late seventies at the time of the meeting.

It is known and recorded that multiple groups were undertaking 'covert' or 'clandestine operations', in particular, transporting agents. These groups may or may not have had connections with either the SOE or SIS. There are numerous stories of vessels disguising themselves as fishing boats or merchant vessels and flying foreign flags. Coastal Forces regularly transported agents or undertook what could be described as 'Special Operations'. A story was even found of MTB *243*, when operating out of Komiza in 1943, having its torpedo tubes removed to carry extra fuel and delivering spies or saboteurs to a point among the islands.

It must also be said that most information of Coastal Forces' involvement in transporting agents or being involved in special operations comes from personal accounts and not from official documents or records. Although documents and Ship's Logs may have existed, many have been lost to time. In most of the Coastal Forces stories in which vessels undertake clandestine missions, the operation is carried out by the ship's existing crew and is an extension of duties of that vessel. This differs somewhat from my father's story, whereby the crew is secretly assembled for each operation.

Some references were found that referred to the alleged mission to Ireland, however, it was to deny that these events ever occurred and to refute that Cork Harbour was ever used to refuel German U-Boats. The World War Two secret files have all been declassified and, while accepting the loss and destruction of files, one might still have anticipated the Cork Harbour mission, if it occurred, to have received a mention despite its sensitivity.

The other mission that you may have expected to appear in the history books, or be part of survivor's war accounts, was the targeting of a French Resistance Marquis leader. Again, the research revealed another blank, however events were found that contained some of the key elements underpinning the motive for the mission as described by the *brown-eyed Wren*.

In 1943, Jean Moulin was tasked with uniting the various resistance groups to form the National Council of Resistance. On the 21st June 1943, he was betrayed to the Gestapo and died a month later. Who betrayed Jean Moulin has been subject to much speculation and, despite several prominent theories, which include betrayal by elements within the resistance, it remains unknown. Throughout 1943, and in the lead up to the invasion of Europe, the SOE and Office of Strategic Service (OSS), which was the United States Intelligence Agency formed during World War Two, wanted closer, perhaps influential relationships with the resistance. You would have anticipated that a coordinated and reliable resistance, free from informers, would be important to allied planning. However, my limited research was unable to identify any prominent resistance leader being killed around the alleged time of the mission in 1944.

The special operations were, in part, from a place called 'Cliff' near the junction of the river Fowey and river Lerryn in Cornwall. Fowey was used as a Coastal Forces base and boats were used from there to transport operatives or agents to Europe. The SOE were also operating from Falmouth and the river Helford Cornwall, where they had many vessels. These vessels were manned by Navy personnel and both Helford and Falmouth,

Cornwall are not far from Fowey. However, no record or stories were found for an operations centre at 'Cliff'.

In his National Archive interview, my father talks of Falmouth, but still meeting in a place called Cliff. A place called Cliff does exist and its location is as described in the memoir notes. Cliff is a tiny hamlet made up of just a handful of properties at the end of a no-through country lane. It sits on the east bank of the River Fowey, opposite Golant, about three miles from the sea.

My father recounted, when travelling to Cliff, catching the train to a place called Lostwithiel. Lostwithiel is a town in Cornwall at the head of the estuary of the river Fowey and is the nearest station to the area in question. It is unlikely that you would catch a train to Lostwithiel if your intended destination was either Falmouth or the Helford River.

The term Z force, or a derivative thereof, was referred to on several occasions in the memoirs. Z force was at times another name used for the SOE (or specific SOE operations) and sometimes the Special Intelligence Services (SIS), also known as MI5. It was estimated by war's end, that the SOE were supporting one million operatives worldwide. Z force also refers to other World War Two special operation groups and, in particular, Australian Commandos. It is quite likely that teams undertaking special operation, linked or not linked to SOE, may have officially or unofficially called themselves all sort things.

The Force Z or Z Force referred to during his school days is impossible to corroborate but this, however, does not mean that it wasn't true. The extracurricular school time activities appear, in the story at least, to be the link, or a link, to the special operation duties undertaken during World War Two.

It is the sinking of MTB *243*, which was to be the catalyst that shaped the future of Laurence Biggs. Although already a religious man, it is the conversation with God that night in the North Sea, which cements a promise for a life and person he is determined to be.

The Certificate of Service has him transferring to MTB *243* on 6th September 1944, until March 1945. However, while searching for the story of MTB *243* and that night in December 1944, I was to discover that, along with some other contradictions, on balance MTB *243* did not exist at that time. It appears it was sunk in the Mediterranean in 1943, or perhaps 1944, but on either account, it did not return to the United Kingdom. This would make it difficult, if not impossible, for him to have served on this vessel.

It is his story that he served on both MTB *243* and ML *243* and, while it is conceivable that his Certificate of Service confused these two vessels, it would however, seem highly unlikely that Laurence Biggs would himself report serving on MTB *243* unless he spent some time on this vessel, as implausible as this may seem.

As MTB *243* was central to *our* story and *his* journey to Christ, I spent considerable time investigating this vessel. The further inquiries however, rather than shedding new light, like some whodunit thriller, only served to confuse. I was left with a shroud of mystery, contradictions and ambiguity about the truth.

The last recorded Commander for MTB *243*, is John Collins from 25th March 1943 to 6th September 1944. Perchance or not, John Collins ceases command on the 6th September 1944, the same day Laurence Biggs, according to his war records, transfers to the vessel.

According to the Royal Navy Coastal Forces Veterans' web database, MTB *243* was worn out, decommissioned and sunk as a target on *22nd August 1944* in the Mediterranean. The August 1944 date is also supported by Wikipedia's 'List of Ship Wrecks'. However, according to the Naval History.Net, archived by British Library, US Library of Congress and the Bavarian State Library, MTB *243* is damaged and then sunk as a target in *July 1945*. This date is also supported by the book, *British Motor Torpedo Boats 1939-45 1939-45* by Angus Konstam, Osprey Publishing.

To further the investigation, I joined the *Coastal Forces Veterans' forum site United Kingdom*. My queries about MTB *243*, returned a categorical 'sunk in the Mediterranean'. On balance, I had to concluded that, MTB *243* which served in the Mediterranean was unlikely to be in service in Britain in September 1944.

Searching for a photograph of MTB *243*, I was to meet Peter Bickmore BEM, then aged about 89 years of age. He served on MTB *243* where he was awarded the British Empire Medal. The final part of this book is Peter Bickmore's story. It is an account of his time on MTB *243* until June 1944, when, according to him, she was stripped of her torpedo tubes and an Italian 20mm Breda gun was installed on the forecastle for use as Special Services operations vessel.

According to the memoir notes, Laurence Biggs is 'Mentioned in Despatches' (MiD) following that night in December. Under the Medals and Awards section of the Certificate of Service, Laurence Biggs is recorded as being MiD and the Oak Leaves appear on his medal cluster. Fortunately, a full listing of all World War Two medal recipients plus those 'Mentioned in Despatches' is contained within the authoritative 'Honour the Navies' and companion volume 'Honour Those Mentioned'. When 'Mentioned in Despatches' a description is noted as to the event or reason for the award. A search for Laurence Biggs in those authoritative texts found no record. Some further inquiries, whereby a copy of the Certificate of Service was provided, returned the following response: *"We are unable to explain how this could be".*

My investigation so far had resulted in no ship and no MiD. The MiD mystery was a greater setback than the MTB number because it should have corroborated the sinking in the North Sea. Instead I was left with more questions as the absence of the MiD from the records and a ship which, according to some sources was already out of service, contrary to the Certificate of Service.

The Certificate of Service did, if it can be believed, show that he was on North Sea duties in December 1944. He was stationed at HMS *Wildfire*, a Royal Navy shore base for Coastal Forces operating in the North Sea.

Understanding my father's journey to a life of service, which started in the freezing waters of the North Sea that December in 1944, was a growing mystery. According to the memoirs, when the ship sinks all hands but three are lost. This led me to search the Royal Navy casualty list. A search for December 1944, found no reports for either MTB *243*, or ML *243*. A search of the data base for all Coastal Forces deaths around December 1944, found no obvious alternative vessel. Expanding the search, I found no casualty listings for MTB *243* or ML *243* for all of 1944.

Not only could I not find the sinking but, if Jock was killed, it was not recorded on the casualty data base, it happened while on another ship, or it did not happen. If only we knew which one.

One to two years before his death in 2005, Laurence Biggs was having minor strokes. Although he continued to function quite well until his death, memories and events became, at times, confused. In 2004, thirteen months before his death, he was interviewed for the 'Australians at War Archive'. In reviewing the transcript, some of his memories of actual events, while containing similar elements and themes to his earlier stories and memoirs, now appeared to include errors, including dates. The flow of the interview was often disjointed and lacking in clarity which, even taking the passage of time into consideration, is not as one might expect. He recounts, for example, being on an Arctic Convoy in 1942 with many ships lost. His earlier notes however, recall the convoy to Murmansk in 1943, with almost no ships lost, which appears historically more accurate and in accord with his service record.

The War Archive interview was now his memory of those events. However, they appear to be an amalgamation of his experiences and the experiences of others. The War Archive interview then, at least initially, did not seem a useful resource in uncovering the story. The interview does, however, help explain why in those closing years, his memories, the distress of war and the importance of God became more pronounced.

The promise to God, a promise he fulfilled as an Anglican minister, is the real story of Laurence Biggs. With the investigation having come to a complete stand still I returned with some hesitation to the National Archive interview and the reference to the commander of '*243*' (he appears confused between ML and MTB *243*) as 'Ford.' The notation for the MiD on his Certificate of Service is signed by a Lieutenant Commander H.P. Ford. I had already performed a desktop search for H.P. Ford on a website called 'World War 2 Unit History and Officers List, Royal Navy Officers and their Commands in World War Two', and come up with nothing. With Lieutenant Commander, H.P. Ford appearing on his service record, I was confident that he existed and, at this point, he was my only lead. Was Ford, the

Commander of *243*, as mentioned in the National Archive interview the same Ford who signs the MiD? A further long and tedious search of the website found no Commander record for ML *243*.

What then had started as curiosity and some rudimentary research was proving now not to be enough. The promise to God and that night in December, was in many ways inseparable from the identity of Laurence Biggs and from what I knew and understood of my father. The mystery of the North Sea was not easily going to give up its secrets.

Then, at last a break through, H.P. Ford was the Commander of ML *243*.

```
M.L. 243.
Tempy. Lieut.,  ⎫ H. P. Ford................... 23 Nov 43
   R.N.V.R.    ⎬    (In Command)
Tempy. Act.     ⎪
  Sub-Lieut.,   ⎬ G. Poskitt..................... 22 Oct 44
   R.N.V.R.    ⎭
```

According to the story, the Commander of *243* received the Distinguished Service Cross (DSC) or Distinguished Service Medal (DSM) for his actions. If Laurence Biggs was on ML *243*, H.P. Ford's military decorations should record the incident. Perhaps now the North Sea was about to divulge its secrets, but I was again to be disappointed.

Temporary Lieutenant Harry Philip Ford, Commander ML *243*, 23rd November 1943, born 16th October 1915, died May 2004, Salisbury, Wiltshire, England, was mentioned in despatches on the

11th December 1945 for winding up operations in Europe. No DSC, DSM or MiD for actions in the North Sea in 1944.

I was then to gain some additional information about ML *243* from the Coastal Forces Veterans Forum which included that ML *243* survived the war and was deposed of in 1946.

The known Crew of ML 243 were:
>TLt Harry Philip Ford Commanding Officer MiD 1945
>TSLT G Poskitt RNVR
>TLSea John Edwin Oakley D/MD/X2958
>Tel William Lunn C/JX262933 MiD New Year Honours 1946 &
>George Garey

If Laurence Biggs was on ML *243* and not MTB 243 in December 1944, nothing I have found shows that it was severely damaged or that all but three of its crew lost their lives. The memoirs do however, say that he transfers to ML *243* after the loss of MTB *243*, which is more consistent with the Certificate of Service albeit that MTB *243* did not appear to be in service at the time. However, the mysterious MiD is signed by H.P. Ford, the Commander of ML *243,* as is his torpedo training on the 14th August 1944. Unless there are two H.P. Fords, which is possible but not probable, it is more likely that he was on ML *243* than not.

A chance discovery at my brother's home revealed an old case containing World War Two photographs with some handwritten comments on the back, the time frame for writing those comments is not known. In the find was a photograph of an MTB and on the back, was written '*243*' and the following text:

>'Lost Dec 1944 – Salved to be a total constructive loss.'

These comments implied that the photo was of MTB *243*. In keeping with the contradictions and mystery, the back of the photograph also said the picture was of MTB's of the *522* to *537* class. A further note accompanying the photo adds that MTB *243* normally had a complement of sixteen but that, on the day of loss, it was carrying an additional ten crew being special duty operatives.

The next task was then to determine if the photograph was of MTB *243*, or an MTB of the *522* to *537* class or neither. If it was of MTB *243* it would be some proof that it was not sunk in the Mediterranean and may have been in operation in December 1944.

As mentioned before, a Coast Forces forum inquiry led me to a surviving World War Two sailor, Peter Bickmore BEM, who served on MTB *243*. He had a photograph of MTB *243*. The picture in the old case was not of MTB *243*, but in keeping with the ambiguity, it was most likely of MTB *528*. The back of the photograph was then both right and wrong.

Other photographs found in the old case did corroborate other parts of his story and I was now confident that he was at Walcheren in November 1944. However, on the back of one of the Walcheren photographs, were the words '*taken from MTB 243*'. The notation goes on to say that the photograph was of ML *917*, and that it was lost a few hours later. My research indicates that it was ML *916* which was lost and not ML *917*.

What is certain, if he did not serve on MTB *243*, by the time he was writing on the back of the photographs, he believed he was on this vessel, a belief that stayed with him until his death.

The final chapter in his military history was serving on MTB *5003*. He did this, according to his Certificate of Service, from August 1945, until discharge in September 1946. Among his possessions were photographs of MTB *5003* and photographs saying they were taken from MTB *5003*. He also had in his possessions a letter from the Ex-Commander of *5003* written many years after the war. Both my father and mother met the Ex-Commander of MTB *5003* when he was holidaying in Australia. I am as confident as one can be that this part of the Certificate of Service and the memoir notes are accurate.

The Certificate of Service, many of which are now lost, is a primary source document in piecing together a person's military history. On this journey, I found that the various World War Two forum sites are full of people who, while searching for relatives' military involvement, report significant discrepancies with the source material. It was not uncommon for a Certificate of Service to have a person stationed at a shore depot, yet in the medal section they receive the Atlantic Star, meaning they had served on ships in those theatres of war, yet the names of those ships were never recorded. It was also not uncommon for a Certificate of Service to record a person as an accountant stationed at one of the Royal Navy shore bases, when in actuality they were working at the top-secret Bletchley Park as code breakers. Further, it was not uncommon that people, searching for information on relatives who had died, were unable to find them listed in the casualty database.

Of the material that I examined, the only true conclusion is that errors exist and, despite people's best efforts, gaps and discrepancies persist. Time has seen the loss and destruction of a great many official records. This can make the tracing of specific details particularly challenging.

MTB *243* – Photograph courtesy of Peter Bickmore BEM

Believed to be MTB *528*

MTB/MGB   222 - 245 6 LOST
VOSPER TYPE RE BUILD, NEW 522 - 537   49 TONS
72½' LONG x 19½'
4050 B.HP
or 4800 BHP
ROLLS-ROYCE or PACKARD ROLLS
SPEED   40 KNOTS   =   44 MPH   or 68 KPH

LOST DEC 1944 - SALVED TO BE TOTAL CONSTRUCTVE LOSS
COMPLEMENT 16 + 10 ie 26 DAY OF LOSS
23 LOST THEIR LIVES

L W BIGGS SERVED ON THIS SHIP UNTIL IT WAS LOST

Rear of photograph

Copy of a hand-written note on the back of a photograph of MTB *917* taken in November 1944 - by Laurence Biggs.

A B CLASS M.L 917
AT THE LANDINGS ON WALCHERON
IN THE SCHELDT NETHLANDS.
THIS A BATTLE PHOTO (YOU CANT HEAR
THE GUNS) ML 917 WAS LOST A
FEW HOURS LATER WITH ALL HANDS.
SHE HIT A MINE. 700 MEN OF
THE RN LOST THEIR LIVES IN ONE
SHORT BATTLE BUT THE PORT OF
ANTWARP WAS OPENED TO LARGE
CARGO SHIPS. THE ALLIES NEEDED
THE PORT AS SUPPLIES WERE VERY
SHORT. THE PHOTO WAS TAKEN
FROM M.T.B 243 WHICH WAS LOST
FOUR WEEKS LATER ALL BUT
3 LOST THEIR LIVES (ANOTHER MINE)

Chapter Fifteen

The Question

What do we know?

Laurence Biggs saw active service in World War Two in the Royal Navy from 1942 to 1946. He served on the Russian convoys in 1943 and was an instructor.

He was selected for officer training which he did not complete. It is possible that he encountered the SIS or something similar during his final school years and this continued in some form throughout the war - but this cannot be confirmed.

There is some supporting evidence for the belief that he was involved in special operations while also an instructor. However, the accuracy of the stories and his actual involvement remain unclear. We know that a place called Cliff exists and that it was ideally located.

If the stories of Ireland and the French Resistance are in part correct, and these two missions were indicative of the team's activities. The secrecy surrounding his operations group may be understandable, as the mission objectives seem as much political as military.

With some confidence, we know that he was attached to Coastal Forces, was injured at the Walcheren landings and was, likely on North Sea duties in and around December 1944. The mystery remains however on what ship, and which ship, if any, sank after hitting a mine with all hands but three lost. The answers should have been found through the MiD but that too is a mystery. The awarding of the MiD appears to be signed on his Certificate of Service albeit undated, yet neither he or the MiD appear in the reference material. We cannot then, with any confidence, say that he was or was not MiD.

From the Certificate of Service to the inscriptions on the back of old photographs, there is a consistent and repeated reference to MTB *243*. From speaking to his sister Edna Collings, now ninety-two years of age, and his wife Pat, their earliest recollections are of MTB *243* sinking and a promise to God made in the North Sea. It seems likely that MTB *243* was either sunk as a target in August 1944 or July 1945. However, based on Peter Bickmore's account, we know MTB *243* was in June 1944 modified for special operation duties and has a gun mounted on its forecastle. This evidence when combined with the historical discrepancies as to when MTB 243 was decommissioned – the possibility that MTB 243 returned to the UK for 'Special Operations' cannot be totally discounted.

Choosing now not to distinguish between MTB and ML *243*, it is reasonable to assume that, at the time of writing and recalling his war experiences, he believed or he wanted us to believe that he served on *243*, it sank and all hands but three were lost.

In the end, the actual ship is immaterial. What is of interest are the events, which in part, contributed to his decision to become a priest. With no ship and no matching casualties for the period in question, I can only conclude that *I don't know*. Perhaps, as the response to his MiD inquiry most eloquently described, *"We are unable to explain how this could be"*.

We do know that he served from August 1945, until discharge in September 1946, on MTB *5003*.

Maybe the North Sea story is just a more palatable explanation of why, after the war, he chose a life in service to God. Or maybe, for whatever reason, the sinking and deaths are absent from the records, or alternately, it never happened. We need, I think, the capacity to accommodate complexity. The explanation may be simple – if only he were here to ask. In the end, like the special operation activities, each of us must make up our own mind and come to our own conclusions. But what is certain, this story became his representation of the war and his journey to Christ. It is our family story.

For those who were the ordinary service personnel and where the service record and authoritative texts are the only definitive document, we can liken it to the Sheviock church notice board. A person's absence from records over the fullness of time becomes the truth, while the majesty and richness of the actual story is lost to time. As hard copy records are transferred to their various digital databases, those who do not transfer or are not there to transfer will, perhaps, be lost forever and so their stories. If their story is told, it can be only a story, but a story worthy of telling.

PART 3
Ordinary Seaman Peter Bickmore BEM

Chapter Sixteen
MTB *243*

While writing Above and Beyond I had the privilege to transverse the stories of those who served in the Royal Navy and particularly Coastal Forces during World War Two. Although it is unlikely Laurence Biggs spent time on MTB 243, the numbers '243' symbolise his journey and story. It is then, with the deepest respect that I finish with a story in the words of, and in combination with, extracts from the Coastal Forces Veterans forum, Ordinary Seaman Peter Bickmore BEM. Peter Bickmore is, in 2014, a surviving crew member from MTB 243 who received the British Empire Medal for his actions on board this vessel.

Peter Bickmore

It would be through the events of war that a belief implanted in boyhood would flourish, a faith and trust in God rekindle, and with it, I would grasp a spiritual strength that sustained me during those dark days of World War Two. After the war, faith remained my companion to nourish and support me, but it would be in those times of doubt and despair, when I was on the spiritual roller coaster that God would walk with me; for which I am prayerfully thankful. Looking back over the past 70 years, I must remind myself that those experiences of war were real; we just had to adjust and get on with it, which turned out I believe, to be the making of what we veterans are today.

Leaving home, the closeness of a large family and Doreen, my girlfriend of just a few months, was a great leap in the dark for me and many of my generation of 18 year olds in 1942. My parents were still fresh with the memories and pain of World War One, where my father had served in the battle of Jutland and now in this new war, was volunteering with the RAF Balloon Barrage Section. Waving from the garden gate, my mother, embracing a telegram informing her that my eldest brother Ernie was posted missing with the Japanese capture of Hong Kong and harbouring the knowledge that, when of age, my brothers too would be conscripted, could only watch and pray as I start my journey to war. With a fond farewell and her words ringing in my ears, "Be careful Son," I put on a brave face and, hiding a heavy heart, stepped out.

Over the next two years my service and duty would take me to places with names that I had only read about and countries that I thought only existed on maps. So, on that cold December morning with a lull in the all-night air raids, I left the family home in Chigwell, Essex, with my little case and travel warrant, en-route to Fareham and HMS *Collingwood*.

I entered HMS *Collingwood* on December 21st 1942, an 18-year-old conscript, to start of my naval life. I could never have envisaged the impact Coastal Forces was to have on the rest of my life. Passing the Guard House, we went up that wide road to our hut where, for the next ten weeks, our civilian life would be stripped away for a military life of discipline in preparation for war. Each morning we would march on to the parade ground for the ceremony of the 'Colours', the raising of the White Ensign and again, in the evening at sunset, the lowering of the White Ensign. It was at, and through, these ceremonies that the pride, comradeship and the traditions of the Royal Navy were forged; the bedrock for the crews and boats in which we served.

As the ten weeks fell away we were moved to the various branches of the Service to which the Navy thought we would be most suited: Gunnery, Wireless/Telegraph, Torpedo, Radar or

Range Direction Finding (RDF), as it was then known, and for which I was selected. It was a three-week course on the Isle of Man at HMS *Valkyrie* with the then secret weapon, followed by practical training on HMS *Pollack* before returning to Portsmouth. It was there, at the Royal Naval Barracks of HMS *Victory*, I was summoned to the drafting office to pick up a draft chit (transfer) to HMS *Hornet*, the main Coastal Force base just across the bay from Portsmouth. Upon arrival, I was greeted with a foreign draft to join the *24th MTB Flotilla* in the Mediterranean as 'spare crew'. So, armed with a travel voucher, I made my way home to share with my Mum, and girlfriend, ten days leave before the farewell that was to last two years.

Returning from leave to HMS *Hornet* I was kitted out and given the usual medical vaccinations before boarding the troopship *Duchess of York* from Liverpool on which we sailed to join the rest of the ships assembling in the Clyde. On May 19th 1943, one of the largest assemblages of ships left the shores of Britain.

For me and the other young men leaving Britain for the first time, the feelings of uncertainty, a mixture of apprehension and fear, eased with the passing of the first night at sea. For many who were to serve in the Mediterranean, especially the crews on the 'D' boats and Motor Launches (MLs), their journey to the Mediterranean was much less comfortable than my troopship voyage. They sailed with their boats, extra fuel stored upon the upper deck in 40 gallon drums, from their United Kingdom (UK) bases to their first port, Gibraltar, before heading on to the Mediterranean or Africa. Sailing in convoys of 3 or 4 and, at times escorted by a trawler, they first had to cross the North Atlantic and then the Bay of Biscay, avoiding German air patrols in weather and conditions that those boats were never designed to cope with. The smaller Vosper 70ft boats had an easier journey, being loaded onto cradles and lifted aboard large cargo ships to be transported to the ports of Algiers or Bone in North Africa, where they were joined by their crews.

We arrived in Algiers on 27th May 1943 and our first Coastal Forces Base of HMS *Cannibal*. I was to join the 24th Flotilla of Light Coastal Forces stationed in Bone, some 360 miles down the coast. Along with a contingent of Army and Navy personnel, our transport from Algiers to Bone was on a freight train; in trucks, which were normally used for moving cattle. We did however, have our hammocks and Army field kitchens were strategically positioned en-route to meet our needs on the three-day journey. We were to learn later that the freight trains were also used to transport German prisoners from holding camps in North Africa for shipment to prisoner of war camps in other Allied Countries. You couldn't say that the British military didn't treat everybody equally but perhaps the prisoners were not bestowed the luxury of hammocks.

From Bone, I was to travel to Malta and my first experience at sea on one of these little ships, MTB *85*, arriving on July 5th 1943. As we approached Malta I can still remember the amazing sight of the Grand Harbour, full of war ships: aircraft carriers, battleships, an array of landing craft and other vessels of all shapes and sizes. You could not help but feel proud to be in the Royal Navy. We were not to know it at the time, but this build-up of weaponry and troops was in preparation for Operation Husky, the invasion of Europe through Italy, the Allied invasion of Sicily. Slipping slowly into the harbour we tied up alongside the other boats from Coastal Forces including the rest of the 24th Flotilla and the 7th, 10th and 20th Flotillas who had already seen action in the North African conflict.

For the next few weeks I was to enjoy the temporary luxury of shore based living, in one of the large buildings that overlooked the marina where our boats were moored. Being ashore, mail was finally able to find us and we had our first opportunity to write home, always in the knowledge that all mail was censored. I must confess that much of this story, from the dates to the ship movements, would come from a secret diary that I kept, which was, of course, totally forbidden. The old diary now betrays it age and looks a bit worse for wear. The ink, which was of good quality, has not faded as much as the paper on which it is written. Conscious of the seriousness of recording operational details and wary of it being discovered, I used a certain amount of coding within the entries so, had it been found, it may not reveal the full truth and I could avoid discipline. Perhaps I was like many teenagers and a little rebellious. It would be because my shore leave privileges had been cancelled for not wearing my cap that I was on board MTB *243* on the fateful night to come which would eventually lead to me being awarded the 'British Empire Medal'.

Three days after arriving in Malta, on the night of July 7th 1943, I had my first operational experience, drafted as spare RDF operator aboard MTB *665* for a night patrol off the Island of Sicily. It was an uneventful night and returning to Malta I was not to know that we would be back in two days time, supporting the Allied invasion of Europe. Getting to know different crews before leaving Malta on patrol was a familiarity that I had to come to terms with. Over the next six weeks I was a spare RDF operator on several different boats. I was however, not to return to MTB *665*, for on the night of August 15th 1943 she was sunk by gunfire from the Italian shore batteries of Messina.

My next draft was aboard MTB *633* sailing from Malta on July 12th 1943, for the port of Syracuse, captured during the first days of the invasion. It was from here that the first base was established for Coastal Forces in support of the Allied Landings. From Syracuse, we would leave for night time patrols off the coast of Sicily and the Strait of Messina. Leaving Malta for Syracuse, all the benefits and comforts of a shore base facility were lost, including the privacy of your own space. It was now a case of sharing what little space there was aboard these small boats with the other members of the crew.

It was not long before the port of Augusta was secured and our base was moved forward again in keeping with the front line, a pattern that was to be repeated throughout the Italian campaign. It was from Augusta, on one of our night patrols in and around the Strait of Messina that I had my first view of the wonderful Mount Etna, glowing red against the night sky and, for a moment, all thoughts of war were forgotten.

It was while on MTB *633* that I had my first opportunity to get to know a crew, even though my draft was temporary. Settling and feeling part of a crew in those few days was the beginning of what was yet to come; the preparation to face danger in a bond of spirit and comradeship that would sustain and see us through the adversities and anxious months ahead. Sadly, those perils came all too soon. It was during a heavy enemy air raid on the port of Augusta on the night of July 21st, a night when we were berthed alongside the quay because of bad weather, that an unexploded Bofor shell crashed through the deck and killed one of the crew lying in his bunk. For many of us this was our first encounter with the reality and pain of war, the loss of a comrade. Leaving MTB *633*, the temporary draft complete, I returned to base with my innocence gone, growing in manhood and better equipped for the rigours to come. In that short time at sea, I had learned that it would be tough and with the bonding and discipline of the crew you find, confront and defeat the inner demons and danger which lay ever present.

It was August 6th 1943 when I received a relief draft to join MTB *243*, a 70ft Vosper with a crew of two officers and ten men. The crew space was much smaller than MTB *633*. Four bunks were forward, the top bunk of which was lowered to make the back of a seat. Squeezing past the fold away table was the only way to the toilet. The other six bunks were in the gangway on the starboard side which led to the W/T cabin and the Wardroom for the two officers. The galley off the gangway on the port side was just large enough for one cook to use the two-burner paraffin primus stove with the added-on oven.

MTB *243*, with other boats of the *24th Flotilla*, carried out night patrols in the area of the Straits of Messina, a narrow stretch of water separating the Isle of Sicily from the Italian mainland where I had sailed before. These patrols were at times hazardous; if you were detected you were in the line of fire from shore batteries on either side of the channel, at least until the battle for Sicily was eventually won. It was on one of these patrols on August 15th 1943, off the port of Messina with two other boats of the *24th Flotilla* we exchanged fire with two German 'R' boats; my first real direct hostile encounter with the enemy.

After two weeks, my temporary draft aboard MTB *243* ended and I returned to Malta on MTB *634*, somewhat saddened as, for the first time, I was beginning to feel part of the crew and a bond of comradeship that I had not experienced before. After some three weeks ashore in Malta, on September 8th 1943, the drafting officer at HMS *Gregale* responded to my prayer and I was re-drafted to MTB *243* but this time as the RDF operator. I would also become the honorary cook with all the culinary skills learned from a large family. During my first operational duties on MTB *243*, Lieutenant Chris Dreyer RN DSO DSC was in command but sadly he was invalided home due to sickness. With now Commanding Officer Lieutenant Du Bouley and Sub Lieutenant Tim Collins as his No 2, this draft ended one of my great inhibitions since joining the Royal Navy; the loneliness and insecurity of not yet having really been part of a crew after leaving behind the bonds of family. This time my kit was packed for good and with it I re-joined the boat that was, for the next nine months, to be my home and family.

September 3rd 1943, saw the landing of Allied troops on the Italian mainland and with little opposition, the ports of Taranto and Brindisi were soon taken. By then the enemy ships we were targeting were further north and out of safe operational range of our small vessels. During this time, we would land ashore small groups of commandos to probe enemy defences, while our boats lay off shore in the darkness, waiting to pick them up. After the fall of Taranto, five warships of the Italian fleet sailed towards Malta to surrender. The only capital Allied ship available to accept the surrender was HMS *Hursley*. In convoy with HMS *Hursley*, MTB *243*, with other boats from the 24th Flotilla, escorted the pride of the once Italian Fleet to Malta. This was, for me, a very stirring moment but, with the escort complete, it was back to the war.

Now Taranto harbour was secured we moved from Augusta to our first base on mainland Europe, allowing patrols to be carried out across the Straits of Otranto and in the Valona Bay in Albania. In these operations, to arrive in the patrol area by dusk, we would have to leave the harbour in the late afternoon, making us very vulnerable to enemy air attacks. After an all-night patrol, where all hands had been at actions stations, we would return to Taranto in daylight after some sixteen hours at sea, keeping a keen watch for air attack. By the time you returned you were somewhat fatigued and hungry.

The 8th Army were making steady progress up the East Coast of Italy and with it Port Brindisi became accessible for HMS *Vienna*, our base ship, which arrived from Augusta on September 28th. Leaving Taranto, we arrived in Brindisi to find the German retreat had left much of the port's facilities intact. MTB *243* was put into the floating dock and it was overalls at the ready, with all hands over the side to scrape and paint the underwater hull with red ochre and to take the opportunity to paint the hull in camouflage colours of battle ship grey and a lighter grey. Supporting her new colours, we left Brindisi on October 20th 1943, along with other boats of the 24th Flotilla, heading the forty miles north to the recently captured port of Bari.

It was about this time that the overall strategy of Coastal Forces was reviewed, as targets in the immediate area were few; the shipping was in the Northern Adriatic and out of our safe operating range. The new strategy was to operate patrols along the coastline ahead of the 8th Army advance. At times, we were involved in secret operations, landing commandos close into shore around Termoli; they would paddle their little one man canoes inshore for reconnaissance and we would return the next night, picking them up.

The Allied Command in September 1943 decided to provide military assistance to the Partisans. Marshall Tito and his freedom fighters, with their guerrilla tactics were pinning down several divisions of the German Army in the then Yugoslavia and hampering the German ability to reinforce their lines in Italy to slow the Allied advance. Most of the thousand islands along the Dalmatian Coast were still under the occupational forces of the Germans except for the Island of Vis which, at that time, the enemy considered of no strategic value. Allied Command in the October of 1943 sent a delegation of high ranking Naval Officers to Vis to carry out secret negotiations with the Partisans with the aim of establishing a military base on the island. MTB *243*, with two other Royal Navy 70ft Vosper motor torpedo boats, carrying the Allied delegation, slipped secretly out of the front-line port of Bari, Italy, crossed the Adriatic and entered the harbour of Vis in complete darkness.

As we arrived, a feeling of unease and an unexpected fear hung over me. In the blackness, we tied up alongside the jetty where we were surrounded by khaki clad figures with forage caps square on their heads, emblazoned with the red star. They looked most menacing; rifles were at the ready, ammunition belts hung around their waists and they were speaking a language we could not understand. You could only hope the negotiations would go well because, to show no sign of hostility, we were not at action stations; my only thought was, *"Hopefully they will be on our side"*.

Our negotiating officers were led, perhaps escorted, ashore for the meeting. We could only wait, remaining on our boats, under guard and with our movement restricted. After some hours, the officers returned and, with a positive outcome from the talks, the tension eased. Just before daybreak, and in order not to reveal our presence to the enemy, we slipped quietly out of the harbour to return to Bari, much to my relief and that of the crew.

With the successful outcome of the negotiation, preparations were made to establish a military base at Komiza, a port on the opposite side of the island facing away from the mainland and the port of Split. Komiza is in a deep bay on the western side of the Island of Vis and had all the harbour facilities, including the now famous jetty which juts out from the town. The jetty and the port, with its harbour wall, gave our boats protection from the stormy seas and with the steep rise of the mountains which surrounded this beautiful little town, it was also relatively safe from enemy air attack.

Before the base became fully operational we had to live a hide and seek existence, avoiding detection by enemy aircraft during the daylight hours by anchoring in one of the many small coves around the island. Draping a camouflage net over the boat and maintaining radio silence, we quietly waited for dusk to once again break out and patrol the narrow waters for enemy craft trafficking between the islands. The RN used a house close to the end of the jetty which has since become a shrine in memory of the Coastal Forces personnel who fought there during World War Two. I, along with seven other veterans, returned to the Island and the port of Komiza in May 1983 for a remembrance service on the jetty by a plaque, placed there in tribute to those who gave their lives in the conflict of 1943-45. This was my second visit, having previously returned in 1985 with a group of 150 Veterans.

After each tour on the island it was a great relief to make the journey back to Bari and our depot ship HMS *Vienna* for some well-earned respite and the basic comfort of a warm shower, fresh bread and meat. Bari had become very busy as the main port, with regular convoys arriving, loaded with supplies for the 8th Army advance up the Italian east coast.

It would be towards the end of November and then the beginning of December 1943, when two events in and around Bari would shatter the somewhat more peaceful mood the war had slipped into for me. The first was when HMS *Hebe,* a fleet minesweeper, struck a mine entering the harbour. She capsized and sank within minutes with the loss of 38 of her crew. We, and other boats of the 24th Flotilla, were scrambled amidst the fire and explosions to rescue those who may have survived. How quickly the true face of war can return and you are once again touched by its violence and bloodiness, but this was just a taste of the catastrophe soon to be unleashed.

At about mid-day on December 2nd 1943, little notice was taken of a German reconnaissance plane high in the sky overhead, no doubt enjoying what he was seeing below. A harbour with all the unloading berths occupied, more ships waiting for empty berths to discharge their cargo and a recently arrived convoy of fifteen ships packed alongside each other with their sterns to the harbour wall to await their turn for docking and unloading. These pictures no doubt would have been received with great enthusiasm back at the German Air Force base in Northern Italy.

At about 19.30 hours that evening, a flight of some twenty German aircraft attacked the port. With the harbour brilliantly lit for all the activity of unloading, the ships made easy pickings. Their first target was the fifteen ships lined up facing the harbour wall. In this line was an oil tanker, ammunition ship and the USS *John Harvey* which, in addition to its cargo of arms and ammunition, carried a large quantity of liquid mustard gas containers in canisters stacked in one of her holds. All fifteen ships were sunk or damaged in the first wave and with disastrous consequences. Together with the other ships in the harbour, twenty-eight ships and 38000 tons of cargo were destroyed and a further twelve ships were damaged with an estimated 1000 casualties. Many were the victims of mustard gas poisoning which contaminated the water and, with the oil from sunken ships, made a lethal cocktail for those in the water and for those trying to rescue them. That night five of us were aboard MTB *243*; the Skipper and his No 1 with three crew, including the Stoker. Words cannot describe the scene of chaos as we scanned the harbour and pick up oil soaked survivors. MTBs were never meant as lifeboats and helping survivors out of the water was at times very difficult. That night, amidst the contamination and death, pulling alongside ships ablaze that were likely to explode, we were to save forty to fifty people from the water and carnage.

Following the rescue, I along with others, was taken to the 98th General Hospital in Bari. My wounds, like many, were massive blisters on both of my arms and on the back of my neck, together with very sore eyes. At the time, it was thought that these injuries were the result of the fuel oil that covered the harbour from the sinking ships. The revelation of the mustard gas was not announced, or perhaps leaked, until days after the raid. The hospital at Bari had been fighting a losing battle to explain why so many of the survivors were not responding to treatment and dying. With orders from Prime Minister Churchill and General Eisenhower, a massive security blanket was thrown over whole affair. The secrecy was to last 30 years from December 1943, in order they say, to calm any fears of an escalation of the use of chemical weapons. The full facts of the disaster were finally revealed in December 1973.

The disaster has been chronicled by many eyewitnesses over the years. For me and for those who were there that night, it remains a deeply painful experience and our memories for the hundreds who died has not dimmed with time.

Ordinary Seaman Peter Bickmore was to receive the award of the British Empire Medal (Military) for his actions that night on board MTB *243*. His letter of commendation reads:

> *Sir, I am commanded by My Lords Commissioners of the Admiralty to inform you that they have learned with great pleasure that, on the advice of the First Lord, the King has been graciously pleased to award you the British Empire Medal (Military) for outstanding gallantry shown in the rescue work carried out by Motor Torpedo Boat*

243 after a heavy enemy air raid on Bari on the night of 2nd / 3rd December 1943.

This award was published in the London Gazette Supplement of 11th July 1944.

I am, Sir, Your Obedient Servant

I was evacuated from Bari by plane to Malta and then to the Royal Naval Hospital at Luqa. It was a great relief to be in a comfortable ward, with a normal bed, and to have nursing staff who were not under the extreme pressure of those at the 98th General Hospital in Bari. With a treatment of daily bathing of arms and eyes with a saline solution, followed by a calamine covering for my arms, the body began its slow recovery. It was now only a few days before Christmas and what was, for me, a difficult time. Feeling very much alone and with little personal gear, I tried to push aside the events of the last few weeks to find that the emptiness was overwhelmed by memories of home, family and Doreen. It would be in the words of the BBC World Service "*THIS IS LONDON*", which still to this day ignite dormant emotions and memories, that I could find strength and comfort in home and family so far away. Thanks to the radio and the BBC World Service, I, with others, could share with the people at home their Christmas tidings and our loneliness seemed not so great.

It was during that eight weeks in hospital, after the sinking of HMS *Hebe*, the bombing of Bari Harbour and the mustard gas, that I came to understand that a faith, implanted during my boyhood years and with our local Church choir, was now true and would flourish. As I lay in that hospital bed, injured in both body and heart, I felt the presence of God and knew that I was not alone. With that rekindled faith, promise and trust in God, I would find the spiritual strength needed as I prepared to face the remainder of the war and the life which was to follow. Christmas had always been a special occasion, but from that moment, it became a time to reflect on all those who lost their lives and to give thanks and praise for my life and family. Now in my late eighties, as I prepare to take that final voyage and, although my beloved Doreen has gone before me, when again that emptiness finds me, I know that I am not alone.

> *With God at my side I pray that the memory of happier times will encourage me for my remaining time on earth to seek these lonely moments with your grace.*

With that promise I recovered from the events of the past and on January 31st 1944, I re-joined MTB *243*. It took only a few days to settle and to renew the comradeship so missed during my time in Malta.

Our next move was on February 12th 1944, when we sailed to the recently captured port of Manfredonia, situated north of Bari. With little time to settle we were on the move again, leaving Manfredonia on February 27th for the short journey across the Adriatic, and a tour of duty at Komiza some 80 miles away on the Island of Vis. We carried about eight to ten days of supplies and, if our supplies ran out before our scheduled return to Manfredonia, it was hoped we could scrounge from the various Army units building up and camping ashore on what was a very rocky terrain. The Germans were still occupying many of the Islands around Vis which restricted our movements during the daylight hours, and on our night patrols we were very wary that, in the stillness of the waters around the many islands, the noise of our engines may betray our presence. After a night patrol of some eight hours at sea, watching and waiting, we would slip quietly back into port, refuel from the 40 gallon drums stored on the jetty before moving around the coast to hide away under camouflage nets in some secluded bay out of sight of German air patrols.

When we next returned for another tour of duty at Komiza, it was on March 8th 1944 and, with the build-up of British Forces on the island complete, the threat from air attack had lessened. No longer did we hide in the secluded bays but tied up alongside the jetty. However, for navy personnel, with the Partisans closely guarding the jetty, which we were not allowed to leave, our only exercise was to pace up and down its length. With our movements restricted, we looked forward to receiving orders to go to sea on patrol.

It was on the night of March 12th 1943 when, with two other boats of the 24th Flotilla, we left Komiza harbour at dusk for a routine patrol north of Vis. In the early hours of the morning, just off Murter Bay, barely visible in glow of the moon, we sighted an enemy schooner. Taking the lead, MTB *243* made its torpedo run, zeroing in on the target. Gun fire broke the stillness of the night as our attack began, however our run had to be aborted when one of the torpedoes misfired and jammed in its tube. Forced to withdraw, we could only watch as the other boats made their runs amidst the blaze of tracer fire. The large schooner was soon to find the bottom of the shallow depths of the sea. With a decided list to port, we made our slow way back to Komiza and then the long journey back to Brindisi to have the torpedo removed, arriving on March 14th. It was around this time that, while we were in Bari, Mount Vesuvius in Naples erupted some 130 miles away on the west coast of Italy. Even at this distance our clothes were covered in the black volcanic ash.

With the maintenance complete and the defective torpedo replaced, we once again headed back to Komiza and resumed night time patrols, which now included landing Royal Marine

Commandoes on German occupied Islands. Using the cover of night, in their Cockleshell boats, the Commandoes would leave the MTB's and paddle ashore to check out the German defences. The next night we would return to the predetermined rendezvous point for their recovery, taking them back to Komiza, their reconnaissance complete.

The enemy targets that we had been stalking in and around the islands were large schooners with a shallow draught. That meant our torpedoes were frequently passing underneath, only to explode on the shore. Coastal Forces decided a change in tactics was needed and two commandos were assigned to each naval patrol. First, we would attack our target with gunfire and then the commandos would board the vessel, subdue its crew and take command. We would then escort the prize back to harbour. The captured cargo was distributed between the Partisans and the local community. We became known as the 'Pirates of Dalmatia', raiding and plundering enemy cargo under the White Ensign. But sadly, our beloved MTB *243* was beginning to show the wear and tear of a life in service and needed more and more maintenance and repairs.

My last action on *243* was while returning to Komiza after an all-night patrol with two other boats, MTB *674* 'D' Boat and MTB *84* Vosper on the morning of May 30th 1944. The dawn breaking over the islands was an absolute a joy to see. The sun rose into a cloudless sky and the sea, a stunning Mediterranean blue, shimmered like glass. The three boats were in spearhead formation, the larger boat leading and our two smaller boats on each side astern, so we were stood down from action stations after the all-night watch. The wake from our boats made a trail of foaming white that could be seen for miles, and so it turned out to be. My station on watch was in the 0.5 turret aft of the bridge, so from within the glare of the sun, the peaceful tranquillity of the dawn was soon shattered. A German fighter, swooping down, strafed the leading boat with a fury of machine gun fire. I quickly rotated the turret, by which time the gunner came on deck to take over. The engagement was quickly over as the aircraft disappeared back into the clear blue sky. The beauty of the morning had been lost. The navigation Officer on the bridge of MTB *674* was dead and there was a casualty on MTB *84*. It was a cruel reminder that war was never far away.

My time on MTB *243* was over and, along with some of the crew, we were drafted to other boats; for me it was MGB *647*. After we left, MTB *243* was stripped of her torpedo tubes and an Italian 20mm Breda gun was installed on the forecastle in preparation for Special Services operations, landing commandos around the Island of Vis.

It was towards the end of June 1944 when I joined my new crew, in what was an atmosphere of deep sadness. During an operation on the night of June 9th 1944, MGB *647* attacked two ships in the Peljesac Channel but sadly three of the crew had been killed, along with two Royal Marines. Five others were wounded. To my relief, even in this environment, I was welcomed, not as a stranger or a replacement, but as a comrade, to uphold the spirit and the cause for which their shipmates had died. It was a big step for me, coming from *243* with its crew of ten and two officers to a ship of twenty-eight plus three officers.

With the repairs from the attack completed, MGB *647* re-joined the Coastal Forces actions in the Adriatic. We sailed from Brindisi on August 16th, 1944 for Monopoli for operations around the Albanian Islands of Paxos, returning to Brindisi ten days later on August 26th. After a brief stay in Brindisi we sailed to Manfredonia en route to Komiza, arriving on September 1st for a tour of duty on the island. There we resumed our now usual pattern of nightly patrols which had become more offensive, intercepting supplies en-route for the still enemy occupied islands. It was during the afternoon of September 13th that we had a change in routine, responding to a SOS call from a stranded Catalina Flying Boat which had been unable to take off because of rough seas. Arriving to rescue the crew before they were detected, the plane had to be abandoned and was sunk by our gun fire. With the rescued crew on board we took them to Brindisi.

Our next outing was with three other 'D' Boats MGB *667*, MGB *645* and MGB *659* sailing from Brindisi on September 14th for the Greek island of Kythira, located at the southern tip of the Peloponnesian Peninsular. Our mission was to land a small task force who were to establish a forward base on Kythira from which we could take and land agents on the islands closer to the Greek border, to monitor the German Forces withdrawing from the southern Greek mainland. It would be from here that we would also be able to carry out patrols of Cape Malea and Milos and land Long Range Desert troops on the Island of Sifnos.

Leaving Kythira on September 30th we headed for the Island of Poros, arriving to find a harbour full of large Royal Navy ships including HMS *Orion*, HMS *Ajax*, HMS *Aurora* and HMS *Black Prince*. I had seen before this frenzy of activity in the lead up to the invasion of Sicily, so I knew something big was afoot. For the next few days we patrolled around the Channel of Zea and neighbouring islands of St Georgios and Gardero, but on the morning of October 15th 1944, that feeling came true with the launch of Operation MANNA; the Liberation of Athens. With NOIC (Naval Officer in Command) on board, along with his staff, and in company with the other 'D' boats, we headed the convoy of big ships, led by the Greek battleship *Georgios Averoff* towards Piraeus, the Port of Athens. It was a feeling of total exhilaration to lead this convoy. As we entered the port, the people of Piraeus and Athens gave us the greatest reception and you couldn't help but feel that the war would soon end.

Arriving in Athens we were given some shore leave and, smartly dressed in our whites, I visited the Acropolis and other ancient sights, including the wine bars. To get to Athens our taxi fare from Piraeus could only be bartered by us supplying the fuel. The only fuel available was 100 octane, as used by our boats. One could only imagine what this fuel did to the taxi's engine! It was in those lulls in fighting, the lighter moments ashore, that the mind takes stock and reflects on the hazardous journey thus far.

For the next few days and together with the other boats, we operated a taxi service from Piraeus to the neighbouring islands of Kythnos and Syros; ferrying troops and VIPs whose task was to oversee the liberation of Southern Greece.

Our next move was to patrol the Gulf of Salonika and, after keeping close to the shore to avoid mine fields, we entered the Port of Salonika on November 1st 1944. Lining the harbour wall, cheering and waving flags of welcome, we were greeted by an enthusiastic crowd, relieved that their suffering may now be over. But sadly, the withdrawing the German invader left a vacuum and with no recognized civil or military authority, a bitter power struggle developed which later required intervention by British forces.

We were to spend about three months stationed and patrolling the Greek Island. At times, it seemed a distant and lonely place while at others, the most beautiful place and people in the world. The end came with orders to return to Taranto via Kalamata and Patras. Making our way up the coast of Italy, calling in at Brindisi to pick up some three months of mail and some welcome stores, we sailed on to Bari and finally Manfredonia to spend Christmas and take a welcome rest.

As the new year of 1945 dawned, it brought with it the last six months of my foreign draft, as war was soon to end. After some urgent maintenance and a short trip down to Bari for the customary compass swinging adjustments, we again joined the rest of the Coastal Forces fleet, operating from Komiza. Returning after some three months away on different patrols, life on the Island of Vis seemed a little easier as the Germans had fled many of the occupied islands. With the German forces retreating, our patrols widened, heading further north up the coast of what was then Yugoslavia to Sibenic and the Port of Zara.

The face of the war was now changing rapidly, with the 8th Army making steady progress up the East Coast of Italy. The recently captured Italian Port of Ancona became the home for Coastal Forces, being close to the military action. With Tito's Liberation Army chasing the Germans from Yugoslavia and with the German withdrawal from the islands, the Dalmatian Port of Zara (now renamed Zadar) became our home for the final chapters of the conflict.

On April 7th, we left Karlobag, which is near Zara, for another nightly patrol when we ran into some very bad weather. Hurricane force winds tossed our boat about like a cork. The intensity of the storm seemed to lift the boat completely out of the water and then we would come crashing down, causing a huge spray of water. It was a frightening experience particularly for a non-swimmer like me. It was impossible to walk around the deck for fear of being washed overboard, so I sought protection behind the 6-pounder gun shield. Clothed in my Navy issued long oilskin, a white towel around my neck as a scarf and with the inflatable life belt around my chest, if we ended up in the water, my chances of survival would be slight, so I just prayed. Thanks to the skill of our CO, an experienced yachtsman, and our coxswain, we made it safely back to Karlobag to dry out and take stock of the damage. For the next two nights, we patrolled the area of Pag and Jablanae before returning to Zara for re-fuelling and await orders.

Leaving in daylight and accompanied by MGB *643*, we headed out for another night of watching and waiting. As night fell, the gun crews and look outs closed up for another night of searching, the silence broken only by the purring of the engines and the ripples that lapped the side of the boat. Suddenly a shout came from the look out, "Target ahead Sir."

"Action stations, gun crew stand by to fire," came the orders from the bridge.

"Target bearing, red 045." Then a short pause before, "Fire."

All hell is let loose; forward Pom Pom, twin Oerlikon and 6 Pounder supported by the 303 twin Vickers machine gun open up. The dark and stillness of the night comes alive with star shells and tracer bullets flying in both directions; the noise is painful and deafening. All fear evaporates; this is you or them. It was in the intensity of the battle that we receive a direct hit. An 88mm shell smashes through the deck, exploding in the Coxswain and Motor Mechanic cabin on the stern, port side. A large hole is blown in the side of the boat only inches above the water line. With our vessel badly damaged, we are forced to withdraw and thankfully the enemy did not pursue their success and take their vengeance. In what was a miracle we sustained no casualties. After inspecting the damage, it was all hands to save the boat as we began a slow and cautious trip back to Zara under the ever-watchful protection of MGB *643*.

Back at port and because of the severity of the damage, only temporary repairs could be made by the shipwrights of HMS *Colombo*. The repairs entailed patching the hole to make the boat as waterproof as possible for a journey to Ancona. Declared seaworthy, we headed for Ancona; a voyage that needed both good weather and a speed that would not damage the repair and risk our sinking. On our arrival, it was decided a boat yard on the island of Ischia in the bay of Naples would be commissioned. It was on April 15th 1945 when we sailed from Ancona on a journey some 700 nautical miles down the east coast of Italy; a journey that took five days with stop offs for refuelling because we could not run with full tanks. As it was imperative to keep the damage area above the water line, full tanks would see us sitting too low in the water.

We arrived in Ischia on April 20th 1944 after our long voyage to be greeted with the most welcome news. We were to be billeted ashore, in a small hotel, while the boat was out of the water and under repair. We were to vacate our bunks for beds, a luxury that had not been ours for nearly two years and, together with regular meals from a most friendly Italian landlady, it was like being on holiday. There were however, the daily visits to the boat and the sharing of the 24hr watch by two of the crew for the whole time she was out of the water. It was here in Ischia, on the morning of May 9th 1945, that news of the end of the war was announced. At first the news was greeted by complete silence, then utter deflation, as that mental attitude of FEAR (For Ever at Risk), our constant companion over the last two years dissipated, to be replaced with mixed thoughts and emotions: *"Was the news true?*

Were we truly going home? What will we do now? The war is over?"

It is then, with the risks of war removed, that your hopes and dreams come flooding in; those emotions, the feelings which have been locked deep within the soul throughout the war are freed. It is in truth a difficult time, adjusting and coming to terms with all that had happened and, despite the elation, there's a fear for the future and a sense of emptiness. Yet, with the trust and depth of my faith I was prepared for the journey ahead, to move on.

> *Whatever is true, whatever is noble, whatever is lovely, whatever is admirable - if anything is excellent or praiseworthy - think about such things. (Philippians 4:8)*

The voyage home was uneventful after the realities of war and there was time to relax and enjoy the cruise. I remember looking out at the lights on both sides as we passed through the Straits of Gibraltar at midnight on July 17th 1944 and wondering, *"Would I ever return?"* It was then on to the Bay of Biscay and across to Southampton where we arrived at 09.00 hours on Saturday July 21st 1945, to stand once again on the soil of our homeland.

We had in those days no mobile phones and not all houses had telephones, so it was difficult to contact your loved ones. Thankfully for me, our neighbour passed on my telephone message. I was coming home. The last leg of the homeward journey seemed to take an eternity. After leaving the train at South Woodford station, I had to wait for the hourly country bus service that passes our home in Chigwell. I scrambled aboard the bus, placing my kit bag under the stairs, not sure if my travel warrant would cover the bus fare. I produced two pennies and the conductor took a ticket from his ticket rack, punched a hole in it and, with that 'ding' from his machine, I was on my way home.

As home came into sight, a lump formed in my throat and the tears welled in my eyes. I stood and pressed the bell that would stop the bus. There waiting at the gate, as if she had never left that spot from the day I left, was my mum. A sheet hung from an upstairs window: 'WELCOME HOME FRANK'. I had to pinch myself. *"Is this really true?"* I was home.

It was with great sadness that we learnt, like so many families, that my brother was lost along with other British prisoners when the Japanese ship *Lisbon Maru* was sunk by an American submarine off the coast of China on October 2nd 1942.

It was time to meet again Doreen, my teenage sweetheart, and to resume our romance that had been left on hold for the past two years. Sundays were always a good time for a walk in the park. My diary tells me that on that first Sunday, we met in Valentines Park in Ilford. Our romance blossomed into a faithful loving partnership of sixty-three years, completed with a family of which we are both proud, daughter Janet and son Alan, grandchildren and great grandchildren.

I look back now in my final years, as can so many of my generation, to that period of life which was blighted by war. Despite the horror and sacrifices, I can still recall the times of the spirit and togetherness of men which, along with my faith in God, carried me through those traumatic years. In many ways, the experiences of war became the foundations on which a successful, loving and caring marriage was built. Sadly, and with a heavy heart, our ever loving and truly faithful marriage closed when Doreen passed away peacefully on December 13th 2012. Death leaves a heartache that no one can heal but love leaves a memory that no one can steal. Thankfully I look back on those sixty-three years of marriage with cherished memories for all the happiness and joy that was ours. I remember with affection those times we shared, the strength and support we gave to each other in our times of need.

It is to the memory that we owe to our shipmates that we Veterans who are left grow old, ensure the memories and sacrifices that were made by those who served in those Little Ships are remembered and duly recorded in their honour.   TO GOD BE THE GLORY

Peter Thomas Frank Bickmore *BEM: February 2014*

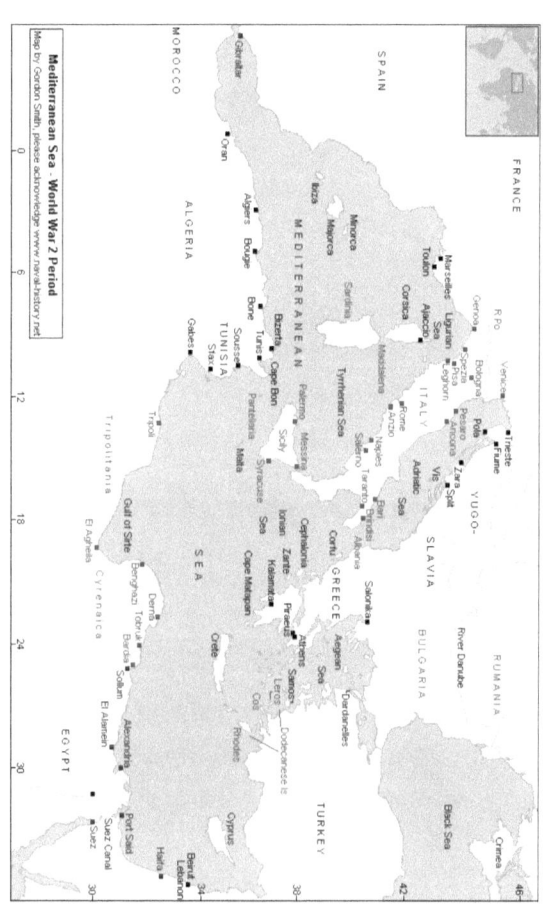

Mediterranean Sea - World War 2 Period

DOCUMENTS

S.—459 (Revised—August, 1939).
If a copy of this Form is required, Form S. 1243 is to be used.

CERTIFICATE of the Service of

SURNAME (In Block Letters)	CHRISTIAN NAME OR NAMES
BIGGS	Lawrence Walter

in the Royal Navy.

NOTE.—The corner of this certificate is to be cut off where indicated if the man is discharged with a "Bad" character or with disgrace, or if specially directed by the Admiralty. If the corner is cut off, the fact is to be noted in the Ledger.

Port Division: Portsmouth
Official No.: P/JX ......

Man's Signature on discharge to Pension:

Date of Birth: 18 October 1923.

Nearest known Relative or Friend.
(To be noted in pencil.)
Relationship:
Name:
Address:

Where born:
- Town or Village: Hackney
- County: London

Trade brought up to: Rubber Engraver

Religious Denomination: C of E

All Engagements, including Non-C.S., to be noted in these Columns.

Date of actually volunteering	Commencement of time	Period volunteered for
1.	2 May 41	Emergency (H.O.)(d.F.)
2.		
3. 15 July '46	S1078 No 175017 issued	
4.		
5.		
6.		

Swimming Qualifications.

Date	Qualification	Signature
1.		
2.		
3.		
4.		
5.		
6.		

Medals, Clasps, &c., L.S. and G.C. Gratuity. (see also Page 4).

Date received or forfeited	Nature of Decoration	Date received or forfeited	Nature of Decoration
	1942/43 Chevron		

Description of Person

	Stature	Colour of		Marks, Wounds, and Scars
	Feet In.	Hair Eyes Complexion		

On Entry as a Boy ....

On advancement to man's rating ....
On re-engagement or re-entry for C.S. or for Non-C.S. after attaining 25 years ....
Further description if necessary ....

1st A.L.N. CW24679/43 of 37 Oct 43
2. " Auth A.B.M. 49 x 23 May 44

Name BIGGS, Lawrence Walter

Name of Ship. (Tenders to be inserted in brackets)	Substantive Rating	Non-Substantive Rating	From	To	Cause of Discharge and other notations authorised by Article 606, Clause 9, K.R. and A.I.
"Glengower"	Ord. Sea.		21 Sep '42	5 Dec '42	
Wellesley			6 Dec '42	8 Jan '43	
Scylla			4 Feb 43	4 Apl 43	
Valkyrie			5 Apl 43	6 Apl 43	
			7 Apl 43	22 Apl 43	
Vivid			23 Apl 43	16 June 43	
	A.B. on Hosts Later	17 June '43	28 June 43	
Victory			29 June 43	4 Sept 44	
Victory		Able Seaman	5 Sept 44	5 Sept 44	
			6 Sept 44	30 Sept 44	
Lothian (---)			1 Oct '44	6 Mch '45	
	Act/L/S(d)	7 Mch '45	13 Aug 45	
Hornet			14 Aug '45	28 Aug '45	
Hornet (HMS 2003)			29 Aug '45	9 July '46	
Hornet			10 July '46	9 Sept '46	"Released class A" SCV/2 on 3 NOV '46

Date	Wounds received in Action and Hurt Certificate ; also any meritorious Service, Special recommendations, Prize or other Grants ; temporary advancements to local (acting) ratings, with inclusive dates.	Captain's Signature

4.

Name BIGGS Lawrence Walter.   Conduct.

Second Class for Conduct (inclusive dates)		Character and Efficiency on 31st December yearly, on final discharge, and other occasions prescribed by regulation. If qualified by service and recommended for Re-engagement or for Medal and Gratuity, "R.R." or "R.M.G." to be awarded on 31st December and final discharge, if not, a line to be drawn across column. Character is assessed as follows :— V.G., Good, Fair, Indifferent, Bad.				
From	To	Note as to method of assessing Efficiency. Superior—above average efficiency. } in substantive rating, held at Satisfactory—average efficiency. the time, without regard to Moderate—less than average efficiency. fitness for advancement. Inferior—insufficient. Variations in efficiency are often explained by the fact that the man had recently been promoted—see pages 2 and 3—and had not gained sufficient experience in his new position to justify a higher award than that actually assessed.				
Good Conduct Badges and Medal			Character	Efficiency in Rating, noting substantive rating in respects	Whether R.R. or R.M.G. or not.	Date	Captain's Signature
Date	1st, 2nd, 3rd.	Granted, Deprived, Restored					
2.10.45	1st		V.G	O.T (Ord.Smn)		31 Dec 43	
			V.G	Sat (y.41.S.A)		31 Dec 44	
			V.G	Sat (A.B)			J. Cassidy
			V.G				
			V.G	Sat (A.B.STY)		9 Sep 46	

Time forfeited			
Date	P., D., C., C.P., W.T.	Number of days	
		Awarded	Served

3. Service.

Name of Ship. (Tenders to be inserted in brackets)	Substantive Rating	Non-Substantive Rating	From	To	Cause of Discharge and other notations authorised by Article 606, Clause 9, K.R. and A.I.

Examinations passed and Notations of Qualifications other than those entered on History Sheets; also, for ratings of the Stoker Branch only, Qualifications affecting advancement.

Date	Particulars	Captain's Signature	Date	Particulars	Captain's Signature
24 Nov 44	Passed I.S.O.I for B. For B. LP & SE J. (T)				
14 Aug. 44	5 Day Torpedo Course	H.M. S. Vernon			

Form S. 1599

DUPLICATE — To be sent to Officer or Rating.

WAR GRATUITY & POST WAR CREDIT OF WAGES
to be deposited in the POST OFFICE SAVINGS BANK

P.O.S.B. ACCOUNT PARTICULARS

H.M.S. Hug...

No. ....

SURNAME (in block letters) ... MR/MRS/MISS ... ALLEN

Full Christian Names ... Lawrence Walter

Rank or Rating and Official No. ...

Permanent address (give full postal address) ...

Date when amount is due to be deposited in the Savings Bank ... 6th Sept 46

	Service		Unpaid Time	Net reckonable Service	Assessable Rank or Rating	Rate	Amount Payable		
	From	To	Days	Months		per month	£	s	d
War Gratuity	21-9-42	15-4-46	Nil	43	A/A.B.	12/-	27		
			Days			per day			
Post War Credit of Wages in respect of Service as a Rating after 31-12-41	21-9-42	20-4-46	Nil	1319	—	6d	34	9	6
			Total amount of War Gratuity and Post War Credit			£	61	9	6
			Less deduction in respect of outstanding charges on pay account, etc.			£			
			Amount for deposit			£	61	9	6

Date of dispersal to leave ... 15-4-46
Date of termination of Foreign Service leave (if any) ...
Date of release ... 9-4-46

Signature and rank of Certifying Officer

Date ... 15-4-46

Cut along this line

If you wish to change the address to which the Bank Book is to be sent, detach and post this slip to the Post Office Savings Bank, 25, Church Street, Manchester, 4. You must insert here the number shown above.

P.O.S.B. ACCOUNT PARTICULARS

H.M.S. ....

No. ....

SURNAME (in block capitals) ....
Christian Names (in full) ....
New Address ....

Is this address permanent? ....
Date ....

Signature of Officer or Rating

Watch Bill No.	NAME	Rating	Non-Sub. Rating	Part of Watch	Division
	BIGGS. L.W	O/Sea	QR3	2nd PORT	TOP

Mess	3	3
Kit Locker	155	
Slinging Billet	H7	
Special Duty	Tels Tels L.C.T.	
Sea Duty	Tels	LCT
Action	~~Tels~~ ~~LCT~~ AIR CRAFT REC.	
Night Action	Tels	L.C.T.
2-Watch Cruising	Tels	LCT
4-Watch Cruising		
Cleaning Quarters		
Landing Party		
Abandon Ship	PORT T.T.	

NOTES.—1. This Card is to be kept inside your Pay and Identity Book.
2. Slinging Billets are allocated according to Action Stations, and are not to be altered without permission from the Gunnery Office.
3. Abandon Ship Stations are arranged according to Action Stations — see Special Notice Boards.
4. One-way Traffic, as indicated by notices, has been arranged to avoid confusion when closing up. These routes are to be followed at all times so that the ship's company may become familiar with them.

Service Personnel and Veterans Agency
Ministry of Defence Medal Office (MODMO)
AS&BCC Team
Imjin Barracks
Innsworth
Gloucester
GL3 1HW
Tel: 08457 800 900
E-mail: SPVA-ASBCCApplications@mod.uk

Reference: MODMO/AS&BCC/1860317/W

Mrs P Biggs
812 Lindman Street
Drouin
Victoria
Australia
3818

Date: 12 September 2013

Dear Mrs Biggs

APPLICATION FOR THE ARCTIC STAR

Thank you for your recent application regarding the Arctic Star; please note that as you have applied as a Spouse you will be given priority in this process.

The assessment of medal claims is a very skilled and time-consuming task involving reference to personal service records recovered from archives. There can be no shortcut to reading these records, as the aim is to ensure that each individual receives the medals to which they are entitled.

We will endeavour to assess your application as soon as possible. However please be aware that due to the high volume of applications which we have received, it may be a while before your application is assessed.

PLEASE USE THE REFERENCE NUMBER GIVEN ABOVE IN ALL CORRESPONDENCE WITH THIS OFFICE.

Yours sincerely,

Holly Bray
MoD Medal Office

Ministry of Defence Medal Office
Innsworth House
Imjin Barracks
Gloucester
GL3 1HW
Tel: 0141 224 3600

MRS P BIGGS
812 LINDMAN STREET
DROUIN
VICTORIA 3818
AUSTRALIA

Case No: 1860317
Batch No: 15162
Receipt No: 699729

Date: 25 September 2013

ISSUE OF MEDALS

The under-mentioned Award(s) have been issued to you
You are requested to complete the acknowledgement slip below and return it to the address above

Issued To: JX392442 L W BIGGS RN

Award(s)	Eligibility Date	Medal Details if applicable
ARCTIC STAR		

Please Note: The award(s) listed above remain the property of the MOD until the recipient is discharged from the services.

Unauthorised disposal whether for financial gain or otherwise may result in disciplinary action being taken as detailed in the appropriate Military Regulations.

INDIVIDUAL RECEIPT   TO BE SIGNED BY THE RECIPIENT ONLY

I hereby acknowledge receipt of the above mentioned Awards.

Signature _P Biggs_   Date _4/10/2013_
Name (in block capitals) _PATRICIA BIGGS_

Receipt No: 699729   Case No: 1860317   Batch No: 15162

ПОСОЛЬСТВО
СОЮЗА СОВЕТСКИХ СОЦИАЛИСТИЧЕСКИХ
РЕСПУБЛИК

EMBASSY OF
THE UNION OF SOVIET SOCIALIST
REPUBLICS

78 CANBERRA AVENUE, GRIFFITH, A.C.T 2603
TELEPHONE 95 9033

November 28, 1989

Dear Mr. Byft,

    I have the honour to inform you that the Presidium of the Supreme Soviet of the USSR awarded you commemorative medal "40 Years of Victory in the Great Patriotic War of 1941-1945".

    Conveying my personal congratulations on that occasion I wish to extend to you an invitation on behalf of H.E. Dr E.M. Samoteikin, Ambassador of the USSR, and Mr B.C. Ruxton, State President of the Victorian Branch of RSL, to come over to Melbourne for the ceremony of presentation of the medal, which will take place on December 19 at 10.30 a.m. at the following address: Anzac House, 4 Collins Street.

    Please confirm your participation with Secretary to State President of RSL Helen Devenish-Meares, tel. 6505050.

Sincerely yours,

V. Kouzmin
Counsellor

OFFICE OF THE HIGH COMMISSIONER FOR AUSTRALIA

CHIEF MIGRATION OFFICER
CANBERRA HOUSE 10-16 MALTRAVERS STREET STRAND LONDON WC2
TELEPHONE 01-836 2435   TELEGRAMS CROTONATE LONDON WC2

Dear Rev Bigge,

Now that your arrangements for migration are completed I should like to wish you a happy journey and every success in your new life in Australia.

We Australians are proud of our country and hope that you too may soon be proud to call it your own.

It is a young, vigorous country, very much bigger than Britain and different in many ways. You will nevertheless find much in Australia to remind you of 'Home' as Australians call Britain, for Australia was founded and built by Britons and upholds firmly her British heritage and loyalties.

You may miss some of the things familiar to you but you will discover in Australia many advantages that Britain lacks, particularly for your children's future. The many thousands of Britons who have gone before you have found that opportunity and happiness are there for those who work for them.

I hope that you will not forget that most settlers would not have had the opportunity of migrating without sponsorship by someone in Australia. When you are well settled in Australia you in turn can become a sponsor and help a relative or friend or even a British family whom you never have met, to start a new life in a prosperous country with a great future. In this way you can express your gratitude for the opportunities now being given to you and also help your new country.

I wish you Bon Voyage and a lifetime of happiness in Australia.

Yours sincerely,

(R. E. Armstrong)
CHIEF MIGRATION OFFICER.

1/70

BRITISH OVERSEAS AIRWAYS CORPORATION

Ref: QH U034306

Tel 01-834 2323
Ext

Mr L Biggs
'Sydenham House'
Crafthole
Torpoint
Cornwall

16 June 1970

Dear Sir,

MR AND MRS L BIGGS AND THREE CHILDREN
We have pleasure in advising that the Immigration Department, Australia House, have arranged reservations for you as follows:-

LONDON/ SYDNEY   Flight   QF110   - Economy Class
departing from London (Gatwick) Airport at 2045 hours
on 30 June   and scheduled to arrive in Sydney
at 0630   hours on 2 July.

On arrival in Australia you will be met by Australia Immigration Officials who will advise you of arrangements made for onward transport to your final destination.

CHECK IN TIMES

LONDON (GATWICK) AIRPORT, SUSSEX   before 1845   hours
at the Caledonian Airways Departure Desk

British Rail operate a frequent train service between London (Victoria) Station and Gatwick Airport. To assist you a timetable is attached. You must however arrange to catch a train no later than 1719 hours. The train fare is at the expense of the Australian Government and you should be in possession of a Warrant for this.

The free baggage allowance is 40 kilos (88 lbs) per seat occupant, i.e Total 440   lbs. Any baggage that you have in excess of your free allowance may be forwarded as 'unaccompanied baggage'. This should be packed separately. It will be weighed, documented and handled completely separately from your accompanied baggage. Migrants unaccompanied baggage, which is shipped as cargo, may contain only personal wearing apparel and personal articles including portable musical instruments, portable typewriters, portable sports equipment, blankets and bed linen. Fully collapsible pushchairs (but not perambulators) may be taken with you or sent as unaccompanied baggage.

Your tickets will be available at the Caledonian Airways Departure Desk, when you check in for your flight at Gatwick Airport.

PO Box 13 · London SW1   01-834 2323

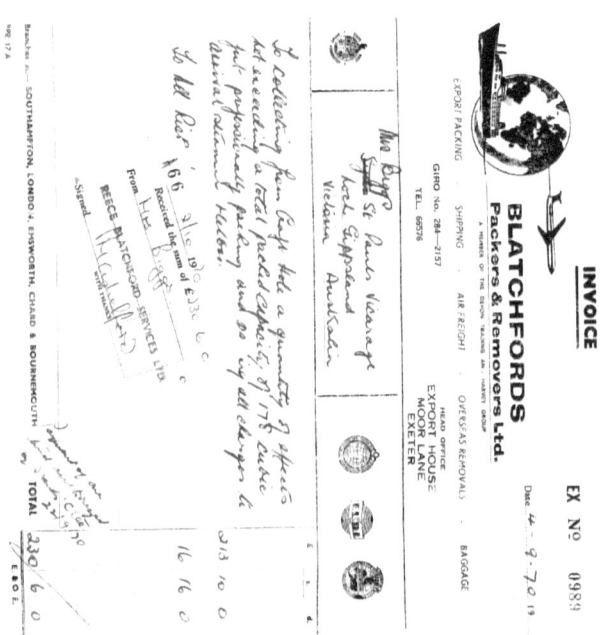

Government House
Canberra ACT 2600

Reverend Laurence Walter Biggs
Lot 2 Lamport Lane
BRANDY CREEK VIC 3820

Dear Reverend Biggs

I am writing to confirm the award of the Centenary Medal to you. The citation reads:
For service to people with disabilities

The Centenary Medal marks the achievements of a broad cross section of the Australian community at the commencement of the new century.

Please find enclosed, the medal and warrant of the award. You will also find a leaflet, which sets out additional information about the award including a guide to wearing and the symbolism of the design.

Enquiries concerning the Centenary Medal should be directed to:

Centenary Medal Secretariat
Department of the Prime Minister and Cabinet
3-5 National Circuit
BARTON ACT 2600

Yours sincerely

Martin Bonsey
Official Secretary to the Governor-General

VICTORIA

BIRTHS, DEATHS AND MARRIAGES REGISTRATION ACT 1996

DEATH CERTIFICATE

REGISTRATION NUMBER: 67193/2005

1 DECEASED
- Surname: BIGGS
- Given Name(s): Laurence Walter
- Date of Death: 16 May 2005
- Place of Death: Clayton
- Sex and Age: Male 81 years
- Place of Birth: London, England
- Period of Residence in Australia: 35 years
- Place of Residence: 2 Lamport Lane, Brandy Creek Victoria 3821
- Usual Occupation: Clergyman
- Marital Status at Date of Death: Married

2 MARRIAGE(S)
- Place of Marriage: Norbury, England
- Age when Married: 33 years
- Full Name of Spouse: Patricia Margaret Cox

3 CHILDREN (In order of birth, names and ages)
- Paul Martin 46 years
- Mark Ashley 44 years
- Claire Alison 40 years

4 PARENTS
- Father's Name: Walter Arnold BIGGS
- Father's Occupation: Lead Mill Clerk
- Mother's Name: Emily BIGGS
- Mother's Maiden Surname: Meacham
- Mother's Occupation: Home Duties

5 MEDICAL
- Cause of Death and Duration of Last Illness:
  - Pneumonia - days
  - Pseudo bulbar palsy - weeks
  - Secondary to severe cerebrovascular ischemic disease - years;
- Name of Certifying Medical Practitioner or Coroner: Dr. A. Foote

6 BURIAL or CREMATION
- Date: 20 May 2005
- Place: Drouin Lawn Cemetery
- Funeral Director: Nielsen Funeral Services

7 INFORMANT
- Name: Patricia Margaret Biggs
- Address: 2 Lamport Lane, BRANDY CREEK VICTORIA 3821
- Relationship to deceased: Wife

8 REGISTRATION OFFICER
- Name: M. Manta
- Date: 23 May 2005

9 ENDORSEMENT(S)
Not any

Before accepting copies, sight unaltered original. The original has a coloured background.

REGISTRY OF BIRTHS DEATHS AND MARRIAGES
MELBOURNE

I hereby certify that this is a true copy of particulars recorded in a Register in the State of Victoria, in the Commonwealth of Australia.

23 May 2005

Registrar

PHOTOGRAPHS

Laurence Biggs on Left

www.ingramcontent.com/pod-product-compliance
Lightning Source LLC
Chambersburg PA
CBHW020611300426
44113CB00007B/595